Does clutter comfort you . . . or make you nervous?

Do you enjoy a race with the clock . . . or prefer a slow, steady pace?

We're not all alike in the way we think, live, and work. And with that in mind, time-management expert Sunny Schlenger has devised ten different organizational systems to match ten basic personality types—in a unique, practical guidebook to mastering your mess . . . and simplifying your life.

"Full of practical advice . . . speaks to the individuality in all of us."   —*Cleveland Banner*

"A valuable, fresh approach . . . can help even the most disorganized among us." —Stephanie Winston, author of *Getting Organized*

"Enlightening and very practical." —Philip Crosby, author of *Quality Is Free*

"Whatever your style, you'll find yourself—and the solution—in these pages." —Paula Kurman, Ph.D., Director, Communicational Judo

"Incisive and informative." —Thomas H. Kean, former governor of the state of New Jersey

"Takes the sting out of the learning process by offering solutions to our disorganization that are as personal to each of us as our birth dates." —*New Woman*

HOW TO BE ORGANIZED IN SPITE OF YOURSELF

TIME AND SPACE MANAGEMENT THAT WORKS WITH YOUR PERSONAL STYLE

Sunny Schlenger
President, Schlenger Organizational Systems
and The Happiness Seminar

and
Roberta Roesch
Author of *Time Management for Busy People* and
The Working Woman's Guide to Managing Time

A SIGNET BOOK

SIGNET
Published by New American Library, a division of
Penguin Putnam Inc., 375 Hudson Street,
New York, New York 10014, U.S.A.
Penguin Books Ltd, 27 Wrights Lane,
London W8 5TZ, England
Penguin Books Australia Ltd, Ringwood,
Victoria, Australia
Penguin Books Canada Ltd, 10 Alcorn Avenue,
Toronto, Ontario, Canada M4V 3B2
Penguin Books (N.Z.) Ltd, 182–190 Wairau Road,
Auckland 10, New Zealand

Penguin Books Ltd, Registered Offices:
Harmondsworth, Middlesex, England

How to Be Organized in Spite of Yourself previously
appeared in an NAL Books edition.

First Signet Printing, April 1990
First Signet Printing (Revised Edition), January 1999
10 9 8 7 6 5 4 3

 REGISTERED TRADEMARK—MARCA REGISTRADA

Printed in the United States of America

Contents

So What's New?

Where does organization stand now?

When we wrote the first edition of this book ten years ago the traditional hallmarks of an organized life were *space and time management*. Both are as essential as ever! But today, as we write this Tenth Anniversary Edition, there have been changes in the how-to-be-organized field—and in where organization stands *now*. With life speeded up and more choices available, it's more important than ever to know how to adapt traditional organization procedures *and* the choices, advances, and changes of the last decade to your organizational style and personal needs.

In the following pages:

the how-to-be-organized chapters will provide innovative ideas for making the most of your organizational style by showing you *why* you behave in certain ways, *what* you can do about it, and *how* you can do it.

the changes-of-the-last-decade chapters will show you how to make your style work in productive ways that fit today's working climate and pave the way to the more balanced, satisfying, and meaningful living people of *all* organizational styles now want.

Let's look at the major changes.

The first stems from advances in technology—new products designed to make it easier to organize your time and space, streamline complex tasks, and help you to do many things at once. Cutting-edge technology is *everywhere,* so having high-tech knowledge enhances your value in the workplace.

Unfortunately, though, today's electronic wonders, which range from faster modems to palmtop organizers, don't come with instructions on how to match high-tech products to your personal style so you can gain the most from all they have to offer. As a result, it's imperative to take a careful look at both the products and your style to see what will serve your interests best.

Certainly learning and using the right technology can save you hours of time and energy. But by the same token you can lose time, energy, and money by being seduced into a more/better/faster technological mind-set that has you investing in items that then end up gathering dust on your shelves.

To save you from doing that, Chapter 2—How Will Technology Work with Your Style?—will examine what you can get, what you need to get, and what might work with your style. It will help you answer "How do I want to use technology for my work and life? What will be best for me?"

The second major change is the trend of searching for balance and meaning that is so au courant. As people organize their time and space, they're seeing more and more that this is only one aspect of living. They're finding that for balance they need to connect with all that's important to them in their work and life. In Chapter 18—Be Good to Yourself: Balancing Time-Space and Life Management—you'll see how to manage your life so you can improve it daily with the kind of balance and well-being that's important and meaningful to you. You'll do more than make it through the day. You'll also get a life!

In combining our joint backgrounds for the writing of this book, Sunny Schlenger, the personal systems designer with a background in psychology and counseling, brings twenty years of experience in consulting, lecturing, running seminars, and coaching individual clients to help them become better organized and successful. Roberta Roesch brings more than thirty years of interviewing people and writing and lecturing about personal development and self-management. Throughout the book the writing is from the viewpoint of Sunny Schlenger, the personal systems designer.

CHAPTER 1

It's Your Personal Style That Counts

I really need to be organized—but I like to do things my way.

Many persons believe that either you were born organized or you weren't—and that if you weren't, you're doomed to a lifetime of mismatched socks and disappearing file folders. Nothing could be further from the truth. Even though effective organization seems like a never-to-be fantasy for many people, you can be organized in spite of yourself when you identify your organizational styles and master the skills everyone can learn.

Common Problems in Getting Organized

Problems in getting organized stem from a host of things. You accumulate too many possessions. You procrastinate. You're indecisive. You don't plan—or you overplan. You're unable to set realistic priorities. You have inadequate equipment or storage space. And when you're frantic about a missing paper, all you can say is "I think it's somewhere at the bottom of those piles in the corner."

Because of these problems—and the situations they cause—it's difficult to get things done. Whole working days go down the drain. You find yourself saying too often, "I know I could accomplish more if I were organized."

Benefits of Being Organized

You *can* get organized, however—and when you have an organized life that's tailored to your needs, you find what you want. You get done what you want to do. You save energy, money, and time. Your days and weeks are in order. And on an everyday basis you live the life that goes where you want it to.

Because you're human you'll backslide at times, and you won't always get to "organization heaven" on your initial tries. But a few failures in the beginning don't mean that you'll fail forever—especially when you have a system that matches your natural habits.

What You Need to Get Organized

After years of working as a personal-systems designer, with a background in psychology and counseling, I have seen again and again that people have different organizational needs. What works well for one individual does not necessarily fill the needs of another. For instance, whereas Denise feels comfortable maintaining a completely clear desk, Carol believes that out of sight is out of mind and insists every paper she'll ever need be in sight. Both experience the same problem of never being able to find what they want, but since their organizational styles differ, two different solutions are required for this similar problem. Forcing Denise or Carol to use a system that goes against their organizational styles would be a waste of time. They'd never use it—or never use it well.

What's an Organizational Style?

By definition, an organizational style is a characteristic manner or method of acting. For example, Kevin, who wants everything to run well, can't bear to leave his apartment in the morning till things are in perfect order.

He willingly rises when the cock crows at dawn to get a good start on the day. On the other hand, Mike, who thrives on last-minute living and loves the luxury of the alarm-clock snooze button, needs a second alarm clock in another room to give him a final warning—since he'll never get up if the snooze button is within reach. They both face the same situation—getting started in the morning—but because of their opposite organizational styles, their wake-up habits are different, and what works for one will not work for the other.

Schlenger Organizational Systems: A New and Different Approach

As I've worked with clients like Kevin and Mike—and Carol and Denise—I've built Schlenger Organizational Systems (S.O.S.) on the principle that most of us have at least one dominant organizational style that comes to us naturally. Because of this premise, my systems differ from the usual guidelines in books and programs that do not consider the variables of individual styles.

Rather than imposing broad organizational formulas and rules, I show people how to adapt the basic principles of time and space management to their *individual* needs and preferences so that each person can become organized without changing his or her natural style. Before I suggest to clients *what* to do, I first determine *how* they like to operate and then give them a step-by-step, workable program that fits their needs and makes the most of their style. The strategies and techniques within each program are simple and easy to follow—that's the beauty of the system.

Because of this approach, this book, based on the S.O.S. program, goes beyond the books and systems that confine themselves to the one-size-fits-all rules. It is the only book on organization that allows people to start with themselves rather than a regimented program or system.

Probably you yourself have had trouble when told to follow standard organization techniques such as:

- Handle papers only once.
- Don't use small scraps of paper.
- Write everything down in a small notebook.
- Write everything down in a large notebook.
- Keep your desk clear.
- Finish one job before starting another.
- Avoid distractions.

Your problems arise because these basic techniques probably are not right for your needs. For example, if you're impulsive instead of deliberate, or sloppy instead of neat, following unmodified standardized rules will never be the answer to your home and office prayers.

The Ten Organizational Styles

Through the years I've consulted with a great diversity of clients—from Fortune 500 executives and successful entrepreneurs to homemakers in transition and individuals returning to school to pursue second careers. They all have one thing in common—all can be identified according to the following ten operational styles.

Time

- **Hopper.** They like to have lots of irons in the fire and work on several tasks simultaneously, but they constantly jump from task to task without ever completing any of them.
- **Perfectionist Plus.** They think they can do anything, but they get so involved in trying to do everything right that they often can't get projects done on time. Even when they finish a job, they're seldom really satisfied with the results.
- **Allergic to Detail.** They'd much rather formulate plans than carry them out, so after they start a project they're weak on follow-through.

- **Fence Sitter.** They leave everything to chance because they have trouble making decisions and worry whether or not they will make the right one.
- **Cliff Hanger.** They thrive on excitement, delay everything to the last minute, and usually need outside time pressure to complete a task.

Space

- **Everything Out.** They work best when everything they need is out in front of them and feel it's a waste of time to put things away in drawers and closets when they're going to use them again.
- **Nothing Out.** They hate to see clutter, so having a clear desk and hiding things from sight makes them feel as though they're in control.
- **Right Angler.** They confuse neatness with organization and believe they're getting organized when they straighten things up and arrange piles with perfectly straight edges.
- **Pack Rat.** They have a compulsion to save because something might come in handy someday, someone else might have a use for it, or they don't know what else to do with it.
- **Total Slob.** They are totally disorganized and believe that they have more important and creative things to do with their lives than stay neat.

What This Book Will Do for You

In my work with persons who run the gamut of the ten organizational styles, I've seen them change their lives for the better and enhance their personal image as I've helped them:

1. Assess their current situations.
2. Determine their objectives.

3. Increase productivity and decrease stress.
4. Win their battles with time and space restrictions in a manner that complements the way they like to live and work.

In this book I will do the same for you.

How to Use This Book

In order to get the most from this book, follow these guidelines:

1. First, write on an index card (which you may use as a bookmark): "The secret of being organized under any circumstances—and in any situation—is taking charge of your organizational styles rather than letting them take charge of you."
2. Before reading the Time-style chapters (Chapters 4–8) and the Space-style chapters (Chapters 10–14) read Chapter 2 to learn how technology will work with your style.
3. Next read Chapter 3 to learn the basic principles of Time management. Since the basics are the jumping-off point for each style's customized approach to getting organized, refresh yourself periodically on these basics for everyone so you can apply them to your style. You can identify your major Time styles by taking the quiz at the end of Chapter 3.
4. Similarly, before reading the Space-style chapters, read Chapter 9 to get the basic principles of Space management. Take the quiz at the end of that chapter.
5. After you identify your style (or styles), start with the sections that represent your major styles.
6. Next, go over the other style chapters to:
   • better understand the people you live and work with.
   • be ready if changing circumstances and situations cause *you* to adopt one or more of the styles.
7. Read Chapters 15 and 16 to learn what to do when

different styles collide and special situations come up.

8. Read Chapter 17 for tips on staying organized and Chapter 18 for ways to establish the right balance for *you* in your time-space and life management.

CHAPTER 2

How Will Technology Work with Your Style?

I'm a "technologist" at heart and technology fascinates me, but it only works for me in moderation.

Regardless of what you've identified as your organizational style (and whether you're a "techie" or "nontechie") the bottom-line fundamentals in the forthcoming chapters will provide you with all the basics you need to get organized *according to your style.*

But along with these basics, another aspect of getting organized is keeping abreast of the latest technology designed to help you stay on top of phone calls, to-do's, memos, conferences, meetings, lunches, travel—and home and family logistics.

As I consult with clients, I find that even the best-organized persons can't keep up with everything in today's fast-forward technology. Neither do most need everything. So whatever your style for organizing is it's vital to assess:

1. what to keep up with for your needs
2. what will work with your style
3. what technology to adopt and use

You and High-Tech—Where You Both Stand

In the past ten years advances in technology have brought tremendous changes to the way we work and live. Today nearly everyone in business uses desktop and laptop computers, sophisticated telephones, fax machines, and electronic organizers of one type or another.

As we reach out to embrace the latest high-tech wonders, it's essential for people of all styles to understand what's available and, more important, what's right for them. For certain organizational styles—particularly Perfectionist Pluses and Nothing Outs—many high-level advances are extremely helpful and exciting. For others, such as Allergic to Details, they are often confusing. The essential thing to remember is that not every product and program is good for every style.

"Will it work for *me*?" is your number one question. To determine your answer, let's look at (1) the pros and cons of the latest technology, (2) what people are saying about it, and (3) today's most popular and user-friendly hardware and software.

The Pros and Cons

3 Pros for Every Style

1. You can save time and energy once you master the technology.
2. You can reach just about anyone anywhere in the world.
3. You are accessible from just about anywhere in the world.

3 Cons for Every Style

1. You can waste hours up-front exploring what's available and learning the tools and techniques.
2. It's easy to make expensive mistakes when trying to match products to needs and styles.
3. You are accessible from just about anywhere in the world (*both* a pro and con!).

What People Are Saying About Today's Technology

Here are some of my clients' views on their experiences with what's currently available. (For a fuller description of these products, see pages 13-16)

Hal, a Corporate Attorney

"My laptop computer is my constant companion," stated Hal. "I don't have a desktop computer at work, but the laptop plugs conveniently into the network at the office, and I use it for everything. My schedule changes constantly because of my frequent travel, so it really helps that my secretary has access to my schedule and can be in charge of setting up appointments and keeping everything current. This way I can work off a hardcopy printout.

"One of my pet peeves about technology, however, is that while it was supposed to free us up to do more leisure-type stuff, it really has had the opposite effect. This is particularly evident in a paper-intensive business like law. There are so many ways to get it just right that you have to try hard not to overdo. And since I tend to be a Perfectionist Plus with Pack Rat tendencies, this can be a real problem for me."

Jay, a Bank CPA

"I like a full keyboard with lots of color and quality software programs, so I want and need good PC facilities," said Jay. "My desktop PC holds a complete electronic diary up to five years ahead, and I book everything in there. The diary holds contacts, addresses, meeting notes, and reminders of meetings and up-and-coming events like birthdays, et cetera. I especially like the computer's abilities to prepare graphic presentations that plug straight into a projector. And since it even sports a CD-ROM, I can listen to my favorite music as I work.

"I also use a laptop that ports into our systems at work. As a Nothing Out, this is particularly good for me, because I don't have to worry about loose bits of information getting lost between work and home."

Rachel, a Research Lab Director

"I'm involved in projects in both my own and another department," explained Rachel. "The other department's staff relies heavily on group-scheduling software to arrange a raft of meetings and events for everyone. In theory I'm supposed to go to many, if not most, of them.

"But I'm so overwhelmed that I don't stay on top of the many E-mails that describe events. In fact, I'm often unaware of their existence, so it's useful to me to just click on my computer calendar and see that those meetings have been automatically entered for me. In that way I have a shot at showing up if I've a mind to, and for a Hopper like me, that's a really nice option."

Tom, a Quality Control Manager

"I tend to be an Allergic to Detail," reported Tom, "and I find a small palmtop organizer works well for me. I use the calendar function, directory/address lists, notes, the to-do's, and the area-code finder. I don't have a problem with the stylus (the pen that allows writing on the screen), and it took me just a half hour to pick up the alphabet. The one problem is that it doesn't always recognize the letters and therefore can be rather slow and imprecise.

"Before I started with a palmtop, I used a desktop calendaring product. The problem was I couldn't carry it with me. Now I interface my palmtop with the program I use at work. This is great because both my secretary and I can track and log appointments. I transfer data several times a day. With this system I always have my schedule with me—instead of waking up in the morning and trying to remember what I have waiting for me on my desktop.

"The reason I like my palmtop so much is because it's the first product of its kind that I've tried that doesn't attempt to do everything. Some of the others have a lot of functions, but I find they're not really usable."

Drew, a Utility Consultant

"Electronic organizers never interested me until palmtops became popular," Drew told me. "I thought they might provide more continuity and free me from the thick personal planners that can get complicated. My favorite planner required me to put in a new spiral book each month. I dreaded the end of the month, when I had to transcribe everything and see how much unfinished business there was.

"A few years ago someone in our office purchased an Apple Newton, the first palmtop. Then two years ago someone else bought a PalmPilot. As I watched him through the course of a week, however, I realized that the task of entering something was a ritual. Characters had to be drawn according to the guide, and you had to wait for the processing. As an Allergic to Detail, I just didn't want to be bothered. I mean, why not just write things down and be done with it?"

Brianna, a Librarian

"My feeling is that you shouldn't abandon paper, no matter how good the technology is," advised Brianna. "I prefer to go with a combination of paper and electronics. I like the idea of having a backup in case something goes wrong or gets lost. And for me, having things written and rewritten on paper is like keeping a scrapbook of sorts where I can see where I've been.

"Being more of an Everything Out, I like working with visual cues that I can refer to easily, so I keep dated daily notes in a student notebook that sits on my desk and travels with me everywhere. When necessary, I transcribe the notes onto my computer. This system works well for me."

Today's Most Popular Technological Products

Electronic Organizers

Planning diaries and day planners became popular in the 1980s, when their creators took the concept of the simple paper to-do list and broadened it to take into consideration (1) the increasing crossover between people's work and home roles, and (2) the growing amounts of information they're required to track. Later, as personal computers proliferated and laptops became popular, the need for products to transfer information from one medium to another became obvious. Enter Personal Information Managers (PIM's), Personal Digital Assistants (PDA's), and Palmtop Electronic Organizers.

PIM's and PDA's

PIM's and PDA's are basically computerized time-management programs that have evolved to handle other information as well. Features include calendars, scheduling ability, to-do lists with tickler systems, telephone and address databases, and information-management functions that allow you to custom-tailor retrieval systems. One of the advantages for Everything Outs who like to print their schedules is that there is now software available from a number of paper-based planners that you can combine with your systems.

The down side is that a lot of data transfer is required if you're using a combination of systems, and Allergic to Details or Fence Sitters may resist the need to do this. One of my clients, Scott, an insurance adjuster, told me the unfortunate story of how he learned his lesson about the importance of transferring data from his PDA to his desktop computer regularly.

"I'm away from my office more frequently than I'm in it," he said, "and when I'm out of the office my days are an endless series of meetings in different places. Not long ago I inadvertently left my PDA behind at a meeting, and when I went back to get it it was no longer there—and no one had turned it in.

"In addition to losing my notes from that meeting I lost some vitally important data I'd had in my PDA that I'd put off transferring. I had only myself to blame, of course, but it cost me hours of extra work to collect some of that same information again."

Some organizational styles find it harder than others to keep up the transfer routine. Allergic to Details and Fence Sitters—as well as Everything Outs and Total Slobs—may have trouble adjusting to a world of hidden information that must be updated and backed up constantly. And Cliff Hangers may procrastinate to the point that a PIM is not reliable as a source of information.

Whatever your style is, you always have to remember that PIM's and PDA's are only as good as your ability to understand and use their functions and be sufficiently disciplined to continuously enter, update, back up, and retrieve data as needed.

Palmtops

Palmtops are the latest favorites of electronic organizer enthusiasts. They can be loaded with digital paraphernalia such as an alarm clock, pager, calculator, notepad, expense log, game board, E-mail retrieval system, Web browser, and even voice recorders. Their greatest advantage is that they can share data with a desktop computer and synchronize information quickly on both machines.

Their versatility, small size, and vast storage capacity are appealing, but it's still necessary to think about their potential in terms of your style and the way you like to operate. For instance, do you want to tap a series of icons to retrieve a year's schedule from a palmtop? Or would you prefer to have a printed foldout calendar that allows you to see a whole year at once?

Fans of the palmtop say that the device is an answer to their how-to-be-organized prayers. In an article on the popularity of handheld computers in the *Orange County*

Register, palmtops were called "tools from the realm of 'Star Trek' fiction to reality." But other people like Drew, the utility consultant who originally hoped they'd free him from having to write in his personal planner, have differing views and experiences.

"One day I was in an office-supply discount chain when I saw a closeout of a palmtop with a mini-QWERTY keyboard," Drew said. "It seemed to be competitive with similar more expensive devices, so at less than $150 I figured I could take a flyer. The thing blew me away at first. It had a touch-sensitive screen and a stylus, a huge amount of software, and even a modem to plug into it. A search on the Internet produced some script-recognition software that could recognize even my terrible handwriting.

"But, alas, my body, mind, and life haven't evolved as far as that palmtop. I still have to travel with my laptop (with lots of memory, hard drive, printer port, et cetera), so I haven't been carrying the little guy around much on trips. Also, I'm reluctant to sit in a meeting with important clients and type into this 'toy' when the keys are the size of Tic-Tac mints and spaced for a Barbie doll typist.

"Meanwhile, my office laptop, sensing my infidelity, refused to offer synchronization with the palmtop without some serious 'counseling' and port reprogramming. My home computer also couldn't accommodate to that palmtop well. Eventually I solved that problem when I replaced my home PC (at a cost many times that of the palmtop).

"Now that palmtop sits on my desk, flashing me a plaintive green light to try to tell me that some date I programmed into it—a date it thinks is vitally important—is overdue. The light beckons, and I swear that soon I will spend a day with the palmtop (at what cost?) and make it really work for me. By then the batteries may be dead, and three improved generations of palmtops will have hit the market, making me feel embarrassed to carry it around."

Scanners

With a scanner you can put typewritten and published text and pictures right into your computer. This is done through the use of optical character recognition (OCR) software. Like all technological innovations, scanning has both its pleasures and pitfalls. For Hoppers or people who do a good deal of traveling and always have to think about which papers to take or where to put them, a scanner may be a good investment. But if you're a Fence Sitter who has trouble making decisions about what to save and what to get rid of, what to scan can be just one more difficult decision for you to make.

Originally people thought scanning would be a panacea that could lead to a paperless office. With everything scanned, there would be no more papers to file. But even with good scanning hardware, a lot can go wrong if, for example, the scanned documents are not wholly legible or an inferior quality of paper is being used. Plus, it takes time to scan in (and check for errors) every typewritten or printed piece of paper that might need to be transferred. In addition, if you have a great many files that you want to store electronically, you need a bigger capacity in your hard drive and, sometimes, a bigger computer.

While I find that some organizational styles are fans of scanners, other say that for them the time it takes to scan doesn't save them enough hours to warrant the investment.

More Options to Assess for Your Style

Contact Managers

Some of my Nothing Out clients continue to rely on paper day planners to organize information in an out-of-sight system. Other have moved to contact managers, the computer software equivalent.

A contact manager is a package with database capabilities that puts your day planner inside your computer and automatically keeps track of such things as your calendar, schedule, appointment book, name and address book, phone numbers, notations, and to-do's. Some contact managers are programmed with message and meeting alerts. When you turn on the alert reminders in the morning, they'll beep five minutes before it's time to do something. You can print hard copies of information when you wish.

A prime advantage of a contact manager over a paper planner is that the contact manager eliminates writing and rewriting the same information over and over. For example, if the to-do's you wanted to take care of on January 5 didn't get done on that day, the contact manager automatically transfers them to January 6 (and all subsequent days) for as long as you want those items on your list.

"Until I got my contact manager I was constantly moving things around in my day planner," said Janie, a real estate agent. "I'd start out with a long list for Monday. But it seemed that on every Monday I'd write down, among other things *Set up meeting to suggest new monthly feature for office newsletter* and *form a committee to plan this year's company picnic.'* Each week I'd keep rewriting and moving those items from one day to another until I finally took care of them.

"Now there's no more of this rewriting and moving. My contact manager automatically moves unfinished items forward each day for as long as I need them on my to-do's."

Other Advantages of Contact Managers

1. All of your information is in one place.
2. You're able to retrieve information rapidly by typing in a key word.
3. You save filing time because you don't have to get out and put back material from various files.
4. You avoid forgetting important things to do.

Financial Management Programs

Financial management programs are among the easiest software programs to use for a variety of different styles. They can organize your finances quickly and efficiently if you stick with them long enough to learn how to make use of their helpful features.

"I'm sure they can," agreed Martha, a Fence Sitter with whom I've been working. "But even though I have one in my home computer, I haven't tried it out yet. I feel more comfortable staying with what I already know how to do."

Martha is certainly not alone in feeling intimidated about switching to a technology that is new to her. But if you haven't tried handling your money through a financial management program, you may very well find that once you learn it, it offers the following benefits:

12 Things a Financial Management Program Will Do

- Track income and expenses
- Indicate where your money goes
- Manage your check register
- Reconcile your bank statements and balances
- Remind you of upcoming bills to pay
- Enable you to do electronic bill paying
- Print checks and invoices
- Transfer money automatically
- Gather information on tax-related transactions for filling out tax forms
- Keep you informed about your savings and investments
- Show you your total current net worth
- Give you a handle on where you stand throughout the year.

Backup Systems

All information on computers should be available in more than one place, so organizing yourself technologically requires backing up files regularly. Developing this discipline is probably the biggest problem for most people, but it can be especially difficult for styles such as the Allergic to Detail, Cliff Hanger, and even the Hopper. While it admittedly takes time to do, backing up your work is a huge time saver compared to having to do it over because of a computer crash or some other unforeseen catastrophe.

Fortunately, many name-brand computers come with pre-installed software that includes a backup feature, so be sure you have one.

For Technology Insurance—The Most Important Safeguard and Backup Rules

Back up all important files on your computer's hard drive on floppy disks.

Back up your day's work at the end of the day

At interims during the day, use the Save feature on your word processing program to save portions of your work.

Back up your entire hard drive every month.

Keep a backed-up set of floppy disks in a safe spot in your office and a duplicate set away from your office so you'll have your information on the duplicate set if something disastrous happens in your office.

Print out hard copies of all materials as an extra safeguard for material you can't afford to lose.

Anti-Virus Scanning Programs

It's smart to have an anti-virus scanning program to:

1. Check for destructive programs that invade and infect your programs, causing ruinous messages or erasures
2. Repair files if a virus is discovered

Some software packages come with a virus checker built into them. If a package does not come with this, you should purchase and install separate anti-virus software.

Are You On-Line?—Try Cyberspace

By joining a commercial on-line service such as America Online, CompuServe, or Microsoft Network—or an Internet service provider (ISP) such as Netcom—you can enter the world of cyberspace through databases within these services. For a standard monthly base fee (costs vary) you can—among others things—find newspaper and magazine articles; research studies; government documents; medical updates; hotel and motel directories; and addresses and phone numbers.

You can also look up topics of interest in an on-line encyclopedia; plug into public and university libraries that have their catalogues on-line; order books; track investments; and search for job possibilities.

All of this—and much, much more—is made possible through an internal or external modem that, via the phone line, connects your computer to the outside world and the Internet, World Wide Web, forums, bulletin boards, Usenet newsgroups, and chat rooms.

The Internet

The Internet is a global network of computers that are tied together into a massive medium for providing information and services in an electronic form. Through the Internet you can log onto whatever topic interests you anywhere in the world. The Internet is also an electronic quick-and-easy way that makes it possible to stay in touch with people through sending and receiving E-mail.

There are search engines and directories or subject indexes that—after you enter a keyword—help you locate what you want to find. For example, a medical student needed information on a genetic disease in which "maple syrup" was part of the name. Along with "genetic diseases" as keywords to start the search, he used Infoseek, one of the main search engines. He discovered the name of the disease he was looking for was Maple Syrup Urinary Disease (MSUD).

The World Wide Web

The World Wide Web (http://www.), a user-friendly method of organizing information on the Internet, is a network of electronic sites that are linked to form a global network for searching documents and transmitting information. The thousands and thousands of sites are connected to each other through hypertext links—words in the document that act as gateways to other related documents. You point to a text or symbol on the screen and click yourself there. To surf the net you need a Web browser. (A word of caution to Hoppers: Following links to information can be both a fascinating and frustrating use of your time. Be sure to keep your eye on the clock and bookmark any place you'd like to return to so when you need to stop, you're not lost in cyberspace.)

Forums

Forums are on-line meeting places that span personal and professional interests. For example, there are Architecture, Legal, Medical, and Sports forums, along with many others that range from A to Z. You can send and receive messages, browse and search a forum library for previous files, and enter a forum conference room where you can converse.

When you want to send and receive current messages, you type your message in the appropriate forum and then check back later for "Messages Waiting for You" responses. This is a great way to get answers to questions from people who willingly share experience and knowledge. For example, Ruby, a Perfectionist Plus and new features editor on a women's magazine, was responsible for conducting phone interviews and obtaining quotes from experts for the magazine's staff-written articles. Ruby hated using a headset and typing into her computer while doing an interview, and she didn't feel wholly confident about using the small rubber suction cup attached to the telephone that the former features editor had used to tape interviews. After that cup fell off too often, Ruby's solution was to go into a journalism forum in her home computer and send a message to members asking for information on options to headsets or suction cups.

By the following day she had sixteen responses telling her where to obtain an inexpensive telephone recording device that hooked directly into the telephone with a connection to both her phone and her tape recorder. (Naturally, she lets people know she's taping them.)

Bulletin Boards/Usenet Newsgroups

A bulletin board service (BBS) offers such basics as a message board for trading information. For example, there's a PC Bulletin Board Forum that offers peer-to-peer support.

Usenet Newsgroups is the world's largest bulletin board. It's a global text bulletin board that contains articles composed and transmitted by net users. There are thousands of newsgroups and electronic discussion groups organized around topics of mutual interest to participants. When you choose the newsgroup of interest, you often discover news you can't locate elsewhere. You can also make contacts that benefit your business.

Chat Rooms

In a chat room you can talk "live" on the screen with people around the world by inputting messages and receiving replies in "real time" rather than waiting for a response as you do in a forum. There are chat rooms for practically any interest you can imagine, and you can get advice, ideas, suggestions—or just plain "talk" with people in your interest group.

Andy, who plays guitar in a folk rock band, found a chat room where he could share his musical interests with others and learn more about what was out there.

He met people from many different countries, and as he developed new friendships an English friend told him about a rock group with which Andy was unfamiliar. He was anxious to hear the group, however, and eventually found one of their CD's. Andy was excited about what he heard—and even more excited when he discovered the group would be performing in a city near his home.

At that concert Andy met other fans who told him about a special anniversary performance in England being planned by the group. As a result, Andy and a few of the fans he met—along with some of his chat friends—are making arrangements to go to England for the concert.

How to Learn to Use the Internet, World Wide Web, Forums, Bulletin Boards/Usenet Newsgroups, and Chat Rooms

1. Study the manuals and tutorials.
2. Go to a computer training center.
2. Enroll in an adult education course.
3. Hire a personal computer consultant.
4. Self-study the many books available.

A Word of Warning—and Caution

Time can be money in cyberspace. To make the best use of the Internet:

- Define specific objectives when you are on-line.
- Set time limits and stick to them.
- Try to work around high-traffic times that can be painfully slow.
- Get the fastest modem you can, because the faster your modem the faster your information will come through.

Six Essential Ways to Make Technology Work with Your Style

1. Before purchasing any products or programs ask yourself
    a. Do I need this piece of equipment?
    b. How will I use it?
    c. Can I afford it?
    d. Will it help me to organize myself more effectively and save me time?
    e. Will my style allow me to be comfortable with it?
2. After answering these questions, compare the features of potential purchases to be sure they will help you be more productive with the specific work you need to do. Seek the advice of in-the-know experts while deciding what to buy.
3. Set up hardware and software properly, and get a knowledgeable person to assist you if you have trouble doing it yourself.
4. Invest the necessary time to learn how to use what you've purchased.
5. Carefully evaluate whether to upgrade and, if so, when.
6. Be prepared to roll with the punches when you have the inevitable technological breakdowns.

In the end, whether technology will work with your organizational style and which of the latest trends to adopt and use depends on both your style and your willingness to be disciplined and open-minded.

You may find, as many styles do, that *a paper system for some tasks* and *high-tech tools for others* is the right combination for you.

CHAPTER 3

Take Charge of Your Time

Where are my hours and days going?

Unless you've been hibernating on another planet, you're already aware of many of the time-management basics—goal setting, time logs, to-do lists, and planning and prioritizing. But since every organizational style will be implementing variations of these basic principles, familiarize yourself with these user-friendly fundamentals, whether you set up ways to implement these electronically or on paper. Later you'll see how they can be personalized for each style.

What Would You Like to Be Doing With Your Life?

This book can set you in the right direction, but first you have to decide on that direction. To do this:

1. Learn what you really want.

Your initial step is to do some "blue-skying"—fantasize about what would make your life perfect if you could control every facet yourself. Take this fantasy exercise.

1. Describe your ideal environment
   a. to *live* in
   b. to *work* in

2. Describe
   a. an ideal day at home and/or work
   b. an ideal year
3. Identify elements of 1 and 2 that are essential to your well-being.
4. Determine how many of the items marked "essential" you currently have.
5. Analyze what this fantasy exercise tells you.

If you're like most of my clients, the exercise will show you some of the essential items you do not currently have. This in turn will give you a clear signal about where to begin focusing your efforts.

Beryl, a former teacher who's now enrolled in divinity school, discovered after her fantasizing sessions that many of the elements she really wanted were missing from her life. Primarily her answers showed (1) she enjoyed being a leader and speaker, and (2) she was interested in relating closely to people and helping them through good times and bad. When she had graduated from college she had thought teaching would fill those needs. But ten years in a classroom—with the constant lunchroom and playground duties, theoretical rather than practical advice from classroom advisory committees, and the endless excess of paperwork that cut into teaching time—had proven otherwise. The fantasy exercise helped Beryl to realize that other career alternatives could better bring her what she wanted.

2. Translate your wants into SMART goals.

In an article I helped prepare for *Working Smart,* the executive newsletter published by Learning International, a sales and management training company, I emphasized that if a goal isn't specific, it doesn't qualify as a workable goal. For example, "I want to be more successful" is not definitive enough. To turn this vague hope into an achievable target, you must think "SMART." Make your goals meet the following criteria:

S Specific
M Measurable
A Attainable
R Realistic
T Timely

Using this as a guide, the previously mentioned career goal might be reworked as follows: "I want to be promoted in twelve months to division chief with a salary of $100,000 and a staff of twenty-five."

3. Break down your goals into do-able activities and identify obstacles to achieving them.

When you know what your general goal is, break it down into a series of simple, do-able activities that, when linked together, will contribute to the accomplishment of that goal. The following real-life goal-setting exercise will help you:

1. Set goals in every major area of your life.
2. Come up with activities that will advance you in the direction of these goals.
3. Identify obstacles you may encounter as you undertake these activities.
4. Find ways to overcome each obstacle.

Real-Life Goal-Setting Exercise

Areas

Job	Recreation
Career	Community
Personal growth	Material
Relationships	Financial
Health	Spiritual

1. Write one SMART goal for each of the above.
2. Select one area's goal and divide into:

Activities   Obstacles   Ways of Overcoming Obstacles

3. Repeat this process for the other nine goals.

The Time Log

A time log is a useful tool for discovering where your time is going, and keeping one will benefit you no matter what your organizational style is. For help in preparing yours, use the sample log on page 29 (prepared by Brian, the manager of the research and development division of a manufacturing company). To prepare yours:

1. Enter in the space marked "ACTIVITIES" what you do every half hour during the day. Use a timer or assistant to remind you.
2. Note who is involved if the activity is an appointment, phone call, or meeting.
3. Indicate what the priority is:
   • High value (contributes to your established goals) + = yes, – = no
   • Pressing (there's an upcoming deadline) + = yes, – = no.
4. Check whether the activity was preplanned and scheduled.
5. Mark whether it was an interruption.
6. Keep your log for at least one week.

Time Log Analysis

A detailed and careful analysis is extremely important. Keeping a log and then failing to convert your findings into information that will help you get control of your time is a futile exercise. Answer the following:

1. Which activities
   a. could be simplified?
   b. could be delegated?

Date: June 8

Time Log

Time	Activities	With Whom	High Value	Pressing	Scheduled	Interruption
8:00–8:30	Swimming		+	–	✓	
8:30–9:00	Mail, sorting papers, planning		– – +	+	✓	
9:00–9:30	Meeting with project team	Team members	+	+	✓	
9:30–10:00	Meeting with administrator	Jill	–	+		✓
10:00–10:30	Wrote letter for Newsletter		+	+	✓	
10:30–11:00	Correspondence		–	+	✓	
11:00–11:30	Read technical paper		+	–	✓	
11:30–12:00	Made and returned phone calls	various people	+	✓	✓	
12:00–12:30	Made and returned phone calls	various people	+	✓		✓
12:30–1:00	Lunch meeting with Project Team Leaders	Project team leaders	+	–	✓	
1:00–1:30	Lunch meeting with Project Team Leaders	Project team leaders	+	–	✓	
1:30–2:00	Edited drafts from morning w/secretary	Kelly	+	+	✓	
2:00–2:30	Conversation regarding organization planning	Consultant	+	–	✓	
2:30–3:00	Meeting on budget for presentation to Board of Directors	CEO Treasurer	+	+		+
3:00–3:30	Chatted with staff about new furniture	Various people	–	+		+
3:30–4:00	Travel between facilities		–	–	✓	
4:00–4:30	Follow-up phone calls	Various people	–	+	✓	
4:30–5:00	Mail, reading		–	–	✓	

    c. could be eliminated?

    d. deserve more attention?

    e. did you enjoy doing?

2. With which people

    a. did you interact the most?

    b. did you interact the least?

    Should you alter the frequency or duration of your interactions?

3. What percentage of your activities were

    a. of high value?

    b. pressing?

    Are you comfortable with these percentages?

4. What percentage of your activities

    a. were scheduled?

    b. involved interruptions?

    Are you comfortable with these percentages?

5. Interruptions:

    a. Who or what was your most frequent interrupter?

    b. How are you interrupted most often (phone, visitor)?

    c. Do you feel that the interruptions were necessary?

    d. Are you comfortable with how you handled them?

6. Goals:

    a. Are there major differences between what you had hoped to accomplish and what you actually did achieve?

    b. Are you spending your time pursuing those things that have high value to you? If not, why not?

    c. What goals do you have that are not reflected in specific actions in your time log?

    d. What activities can you add to your schedule to make progress toward them?

How Do You Plan Your Days to Accomplish What You Want To Do?

A baseball coach once rebuked a confident player who said his team would win because it had the will to win. "Don't kid yourself," said the coach. "The will to win is important, but it isn't worth a nickel unless you also have the will to prepare."

Successful people know this, and research studies show that the more time you spend on advance planning, the less time overall, you'll require to complete a job. In fact, they prove that one moment spent in planning not only saves three or four in carrying out a task but also gives better results. Similarly, planning helps you fend off problems and equips you to handle unexpected developments without a lot of wheel-spinning.

How to Plan

Planning can be divided into long-range, or wide-angle, planning, and short-range, or microscopic, planning. The former concentrates on the total picture of what you want to achieve, and the latter pinpoints the step-by-step activities that will get you there. Here are the important points about each:

Long-range planning

This can range from one to five years or longer, and gives you the overall direction you need to take to achieve your important goals.

Short-range planning

This can be broken up into the following categories:

1. Six-month planning (1) makes you aware of the tasks most likely to benefit you in attaining long-

range goals; and (2) helps you see and take advantage of opportunities that arise.

2. One-month planning enables you to perceive and avoid possible crises before they occur.

3. Daily and weekly planning increases your general effectiveness and builds up the essential habit of staying in control of your time. Day-to-day planning can be done either the night before, or in the morning, depending upon the available time and the nature of your job.

Prioritizing

As you plan you're always prioritizing—whether you realize it or not. When you say, "I don't have time to do this," you're really saying, "I choose to do something else instead." Consequently, understanding what criteria to use when you make your choices is a critical factor in setting priorities.

In the eighteenth century, economist Vilfredo Pareto developed what is popularly known as the 80/20 Rule, or the Pareto Principle. This rule states that 80 percent of the value of a group of activities is generally concentrated in only 20 percent of those activities. The Pareto Principle, also called the concept of the "vital few" and the "trivial many," encourages you to concentrate on the few high value items that will bring the greatest results.

For instance, in a list of ten items to do, doing the two of the highest value (or 20 percent) will give you 80 percent of the value to be gained from doing every item on the list. If you identify and do just those two, you can feel confident you've made the best use of your time—even if you were never able to get anywhere near the other eight items.

To Do Lists That Work

Many people try to keep some sort of prioritized To Do List, but most have not given much thought to exactly how their To Do's should be organized. My solution is a simple process that will give you an overall view of everything that is waiting to be done, and make it clear which items should be handled first on a day-to-day basis.

This process is effective because it encourages you to balance different kinds of important needs:

1. What I should do/What I want to do
   To keep a balance, concentrate not only on what you believe you must accomplish, but also on what could simply be pleasurable, or fulfilling.
2. Things to do for me/Things to do for them
   Your lists should contain items that will satisfy your needs as well as those that will satisfy the needs, requests, or demands of significant others in your life.
3. What should be done now/What can wait until later
   As much as you might like to, you can't accomplish everything at once. Some things therefore should wait until later to be tackled. But preferably they should be the lower-value, less pressing items.
4. What has value/What is pressing
   Value has to do with importance, while pressing refers to urgency and deadline pressure. It's tempting to react only to the tyranny of the urgent, but be sure to also pay attention to the high-value items that may have no immediate deadline but whose payoff is great.

One of the major problems in organizing time effectively results from the fact that many low-priority items tend to be pressing (the dog must be walked right now, the expense report must be prepared tonight, the magazine with the routing slip must be passed along tomorrow). By the same token, the important things in life often have no deadline (there's generally no immediate pressure to make your life more interesting or to develop your talents). The trick is to understand the difference between what has value and what is pressing so that the right things get done in the right order.

The Master List and Daily List

Both the Master List (the running list of *everything* you have to do) and the Daily List are essential parts of planning and scheduling. The sample Master List on page 35 and the Daily List on page 36 will show you how to set them up. Both were prepared by a woman who must combine three distinct areas in her life: school (going for her M.B.A.), work (part-time reporter), and personal.

As you can see, the Master List is divided into four columns:

1	*2*	*3*	*4*
IMPORTANT	IMPORTANT	UNIMPORTANT	UNIMPORTANT
PRESSING	NOT PRESSING	PRESSING	NOT PRESSING

To assign an activity to one of the four columns, you need to determine:

1. Will this activity return to me a large payoff on the time I'd invest in it? If the answer is yes, this is an important activity.
2. Is this activity time-critical? Is there a rapidly approaching deadline that should be met? If the answer is yes, this is a pressing activity.

You'll probably find that some columns always seem to have more entries than the others, whereas some have less. Don't worry.

Month: October   Master List

Important		Unimportant	
Pressing	Not Pressing	Pressing	Not Pressing
SCHOOL: Homework problems for Accounting Read Chapter 5, Accounting Rewrite Corporate Law paper Do catch-up reading for Law *WORK:* Do interviews for jewelry article Start writing apparel company piece Send out expense bills Call Bart to turn down assignment *PERSONAL:* Deposit check Put laundry away Balance checkbooks Do food shopping	*SCHOOL:* Read next chapter for Accounting Read next chapters for Law *WORK:* Call Stempert to set up interview Call AT&T to find out work status Set up dinner meeting for book venture Return religious school book Order next year's agenda sheets *PERSONAL:* Go to club to exercise Buy brother's birthday present Get vacuum cleaner fixed Wallpaper bedroom Set up sewing cabinet	*WORK:* Critique newsletter Call UJC re workshops planned Do dairy story follow-up Set up clothing store interview *PERSONAL:* Get water heater fixed	*SCHOOL:* Figure out next semester's schedule Look into internship possibilities Get business magazine subscriptions Sell off old books *WORK:* Start working on list of free-lance opportunities *PERSONAL:* Plan Halloween party

Daily List

Priority	Call	Write	Do
1. Interviews for jewelry article			x
2. Read Chapter 5, Accounting			x
3. Do food shopping			x
4. Set up Stempert interview	x		
5. Homework problems, Accounting		x	
!6. Exercise at club			x
7. Send out expense bills		x	
8. Put laundry away			x
!9. Start writing apparel company piece		x	
10. Catch-up reading for Law			x

! The two items I will do today, or else!

The important thing is to have an overview of the entire picture. Also, though you'll want to concentrate primarily on Column 1 (Important/Pressing) you do need to build in time for Column 2 (Important/Not pressing). You can do this by automatically leaving room for one item from Column 2 in your schedule every week. This ensures that *all* of your high-value items will receive attention.

After you complete your Master List, the second step is the Daily List, on which you will transfer a limited number of items from the Master List as well as others that come up in the course of that day. As you'll note on the sample Daily List, there are only ten spaces available, which keeps your list at a reasonable length. You can always substitute items if your priorities suddenly change or add more after you finish the original ten.

Scheduling

Once you've made your Master and Daily lists you can schedule your activities into blocks of time. To do this effectively, there are several factors to keep in mind.

1. Other People's Schedules

There are obvious things you cannot do (a) except in specific hours and (b) according to other people's schedules—for example, going to the bank, seeing your boss about a raise, enrolling in a college course, or settling in at the library for a session with the microfilm.

2. Time Limits

A deadline generally forces you to be on time in carrying out your plans—and without a deadline most of us never find the right time to get started! As the late Inez Robb, a newspaper columnist who covered the world and wrote three columns a week, once said, "If I didn't have deadlines I'd only write one column a year."

3. Energy Levels

All of us have regular cycles in which we're highly productive or in which we seem to accomplish little. Therefore, the more consistently we match our activities to our capacities, the more productive we'll be.

Naturally, this applies to the time we can control, because not all of our time is discretionary. For example, if your energy for physical exercise is highest at 8:00 A.M. and you're due at work at that hour, you're not in a spot to make use of that peak.

To learn your energy level patterns you'll want to keep track of the hours you feel physically energetic and mentally sharp as well as those when you're overcome by fatigue.

How to Keep Track—Your Energy-Level Chart

The sample Energy-Level Chart, Activity List, and To Do Schedule on the following pages were prepared by a college anthropology instructor during her summer vacation. By becoming aware of the fluctuations in her energy levels, she was able to schedule her most demanding tasks when she was best able to perform them. To prepare your charts:

1. Use the numbers below to designate on the Energy-Level Chart your level of mental energy and physical energy every hour of the day.

   5 high
   4 medium to high
   3 medium
   2 low to medium
   1 low

2. Fill in the chart every day for a week, using one color for physical energy and another for mental energy.
3. Look for patterns in your scores.

Matching Your Energy Level With Your Daily Activities

1. To fill in the Activity List, list all daily activities and current projects in Column A.
2. Ask yourself what level of mental and/or physical energy is required to perform each task adequately (not perfectly!).
3. Enter numbers in Columns B and C.
4. Consult patterns indicated in Energy-Level Chart.
5. Schedule your time in Column D by taking advantage of your strengths and compensating for your weaknesses as you notice how your energy levels and capacities fluctuate throughout the day.

Energy Level Chart

Hours of the Day	Monday		Tuesday		Wednesday		Thursday		Friday		Saturday		Sunday	
	M	P	M	P	M	P	M	P	M	P	M	P	M	P
6:00 A.M.	1	1	1	1	1	1	1	1	1	1	1	1	1	1
7:00	1	1	1	1	1	1	1	1	1	1	1	2	1	1
8:00	3	2	2	1	3	2	3	3	3	2	3	3	2	2
9:00	4	3	4	2	4	3	5	4	4	3	4	3	3	3
10:00	5	4	4	3	5	4	5	4	4	3	4	4	3	3
11:00	4	4	3	3	4	3	4	4	4	4	4	4	4	3
12:00 P.M.	3	3	3	2	3	3	3	3	3	2	3	3	3	3
1:00	3	2	3	2	3	3	3	3	3	3	3	3	3	3
2:00	3	2	3	1	3	2	3	3	3	3	3	3	3	3
3:00	3	3	2	1	3	3	3	2	3	3	3	2	3	3
4:00	3	3	3	2	3	2	3	2	3	3	2	2	2	2
5:00	2	3	3	3	2	3	2	3	3	2	2	2	2	2
6:00	2	3	3	3	2	3	3	3	3	3	3	3	3	3
7:00	3	3	2	2	4	2	3	2	3	2	4	4	3	3
8:00	4	2	2	2	3	2	4	2	4	2	3	3	3	2
9:00	3	2	2	1	3	2	3	2	3	2	3	3	3	3
10:00	2	1	2	1	2	1	2	2	2	1	2	2	2	2
11:00	1	1	1	1	1	1	2	1	1	1	3	3	3	1
12:00 A.M.	1	1	1	1	1	1	2	1	1	1	2	2	2	1

M = Mental Energy
P = Physical Energy

Activity List

#	A *Daily Tasks/ Current Projects*	B *Mental Energy Level Required*	C *Physical Energy Level required*	D *Best Time to Do*
1	Select children's clothes for the day	3	3	Morning
2	Make children's lunch for day camp	3	3	After dinner
3	Open mail	2	2	Afternoon
4	Decide what to have for dinner	3	1	Morning
5	Do filing	4	3	Morning
6	Make dinner	3	3	Dinnertime
7	Do laundry	3	4	Morning
8	Fold laundry	1	3	Evening
9	Write to pen pal	4	2	Evening
10	Run	2	4	Late morning
11	Play tennis	3	4	Late morning
12	Organize chest of clothing accessories	4	3	Evening
13	Balance checkbook	4	2	Evening
14	Pay bills	3	3	Afternoon
15	Hang picture on den wall	4	4	Morning
16	Decide on birthday gifts	5	2	Morning

#	*A* *Daily Tasks/ Current Projects*	*B* *Mental Energy Level Required*	*C* *Physical Energy Level required*	*D* *Best Time to Do*
17	Shop for birth- day gifts	3	4	Morning
18	Do phoning for reunion committee	3	3	Afternoon
19	Plan party for Labor Day	5	2	Morning
20	Take children to have formal photo taken	3	5	Late morning
21	Straighten house	3	3	Afternoon
22	Walk dogs	2	3	Afternoon
23				
24				
25				

To Do Schedule

		APPOINTMENTS	*To Do*	*To Write*	*To Call*
8	00 15 30 45				
9	00 15 30 45		Do filing Hang picture on wall		
10	00 15 30 45	Margie—tennis game			
11	00 15 30 45		Plan party for Labor Day		

	APPOINTMENTS	To Do	To Write	To Call
12 00 15 30 45	Liz—lunch & shop for birthday gifts			
1 00 15 30 45		Walk dogs		
2 00 15 30 45		Straighten house		
3 00 15 30 45			Pay bills	Reunion committee list
4 00 15 30 45				
5 00 15 30 45				
6 00 30				
7 00 30		Fold laundry		
8 00 30				
9 00 30			Pen pal	

Time-Style Quiz

The following quiz will help you identify your style(s) of managing time. It's okay to have more than one answer per question because many people are a combination of styles. For example, if your answers are mostly

As, you're primarily a Hopper. If your answers are mostly Cs you're primarily a Cliff Hanger. If you have an equal combination of both, you're a mix of those two styles. The key at the end of the quiz will direct you to the chapters that discuss your primary styles.

1. If I have too much work to do, I might:
    a. Try to do a little bit on each task.
    b. Work late trying to do a good job on everything.
    c. Speed up my pace and hope that there aren't too many mistakes.
    d. Waste a lot of time worrying about where to start.
    e. Rely on that burst of adrenaline I always get when rushing to meet a deadline.
2. When conducting a meeting to discuss an issue, I would probably:
    a. Allow the discussion to cover all interesting points whether they are part of the agenda or not.
    b. Stick faithfully to the agenda, covering all of the items thoroughly.
    c. Present the big picture, without going into all the nitty-gritty detail.
    d. Allow the outspoken people in the room to shape the discussion.
    e. Let the discussion run on as long as people had things to say, leaving the decision for the end of the day.
3. When I pack for a business trip I:
    a. Alternate between gathering toiletries, folding shirts, and ironing clothes.
    b. Make a written list several weeks in advance so I have all the right items.
    c. Go through my drawers and pull out whatever I need as it occurs to me.
    d. Spend hours trying to figure out what to take.
4. When I set up a vacation, I prefer to:
    a. Visit twelve cities in ten days.

b. Spend several months doing research so I can have the ultimate trip.
c. Fly stand-by and stay wherever I find vacancies.
d. Take a package tour so my decisions are kept to a minimum.
e. Leave all the planning to the last minute.

Key: a. Hopper b. Perfectionist Plus c. Allergic to Detail d. Fence Sitter
e. Cliff Hanger

A Final Point

Whether you're an Everything Out, Nothing Out. Right Angler, Pack Rat, Total Slob, Perfectionist Plus, Allergic to Detail, Fence Sitter, Cliff Hanger, or Hopper, always remember to factor in Murphy's Law (Whatever can go wrong, will) as you match your energy level with your daily activities.

Keeping this in mind, figure out how long something should take and then tack on extra time as a buffer. You may need it to handle an unexpected situation. If you don't, just "take time to smell the flowers," an important part of being organized, too,—for *every* organizational style.

Hopper

*I jump from task to task and often don't
complete what I start.*

Hopping is the most common of all organizational styles.
Hoppers switch from one thing to another like players
in a leap-frog game. A data-processing programmer lets
himself get diverted because every task he undertakes
reminds him of something else. A corporation lawyer is
constantly off and running in several directions at once.
And an administrative dietician is propelled out of one
activity into whatever new one comes up.

All of these people are Hoppers—and maybe you are,
too, if you catch a sudden glimpse of yourself in any of
their actions. To see if this is one of your styles take the
following quiz.

Are You a Hopper?

As you answer Never (N), Occasionally (O), or Frequently (F), rate yourself according to the following scale.

Never	*Occasionally*	*Frequently*
0 points	1 point	2 points

N O F

1. Do you enjoy having a number of irons
   in the fire?

2. Do you find yourself working on several tasks simultaneously?
3. Do you interrupt what you're working on to do something you just remembered?
4. Do you leave tasks unfinished?
5. Do you find yourself moving in fits and starts?
6. Do you have trouble remembering where you placed items?
7. Are you easily distracted?
8. Do people complain that they can't follow your train of thought?
9. Do you tend to run around faster when you feel confused or anxious about your work?
10. Do you ever start out to work in one room and wind up in another without knowing how you got there?

———————

Totals:

0–6 points	You're not really a Hopper.
7–13 points	You have strong Hopper tendencies
14–20 points	You're a full-fledged Hopper.

Why You Hop

Many of us Hop at one time or another for a variety of reasons. Note the following to see what applies to you.

1. You're easily distracted.

Harvey, a personnel director of a large telephone company, is visually oriented. Like the data-processor programmer, everything he sees reminds him of something else he wants to do. If he spots a coworker he'd like to talk to, he'll drop what he's doing for that. Or, when his secretary brings the mail, he'll shove aside the résumés he's reading to glance through the pile of mail. And when he's partially finished with that, he'll leave his office to show someone a letter he has just received.

Even at home, Harvey admits, he's guilty of letting distractions interfere with what he needs to do. "One night only a few days ago I took résumés home from the office," he said, "so I knew when I finished my dinner that I needed to get right to them. But when I sat down at my desk in the den, I happened to see some new books my wife had put on the shelves, and since I'm an avid reader I automatically got up to look at them.

"I managed not to sit down with them, but while I was walking back to my desk, I passed a row of child-psychology texts that I'd had in college. I began to wonder how textbook theories would hold up against my practical experience as a father of three, so I did sit down with one of those books to flip through the pages briefly. The next thing I knew, over an hour had passed and I hadn't started my work. Simply by nature I operate this way."

If you find that you are easily distracted:

- Use automatic mechanisms that grab your attention and alert you to the fact you may not be sticking to your top priorities.

   For Harvey the mechanism alerting him to the passage of time and getting him back on track was an alarm watch that he set at half-hour intervals.
- Avoid undesired eye contact with people by facing your desk away from the door or blocking your visibility with a large plant or partition.
- Minimize nonessential interruptions by—for example—scheduling mail drops for late in the day.

2. You enjoy variety and change of pace.

Hoppers need diversity and a number of projects going simultaneously, so Jodi, a production assistant at a television station, thoroughly enjoys the scope of her job and the challenge of handling a variety of things.

"Until everything gets out of hand and I'm trying to do four things at once, I'm able to keep up my energy by switching from project to project," she said. "But when I get behind as I am now, I find myself working in fits and starts and not getting anywhere.

"Yesterday, for example, I began to dig through a file labeled 'People to Contact for Possible Future Guests,' which my boss is hassling me to get to. But the file is so full of papers it's collapsed upon itself, so after twenty minutes I put that aside to start working on a list of ten phone calls to persons we know we're going to book in the next two or three weeks.

"I had only completed three calls, though, before I decided I'd better get to work on a speech on television production that I had agreed to give at a workshop for women in television. I started to look for the letter from the person who'd asked me to speak. But after ten minutes of not being able to find it, I moved on to something else."

If you like variety and change of pace:

- Make certain you complete projects by setting up "mini-goals" or specified time frames for each task you undertake.

  For a day such as Jodi described, I suggested first allotting a solid two hours to making a dent in her "People to Contact for Possible Future Guests" file, since two hours would give her at least a start on it. Then she could place ten phone calls before hopping off to a specific amount of time to look for the letter asking her to speak so she could work on her lecture.

3. You desire immediate gratification.

Peter, the vice-president for marketing at a small over-the-counter pharmaceutical company, has a head full of innovative ideas for recommendations on product design and in-store advertising. But he moves so quickly from this newly launched project to other projects-in-progress that one of his problems when he consulted me was locating his rapidly written notes on the product-design project he hoped to work on throughout that day *if only* he could find the notes.

"I shoved them somewhere temporarily to do something else," he said, "and I'm sure they couldn't have walked away. But I don't know where they went. That's only one of my problems, though.

"I'm also playing the waiting game with our operations people because developing a new packaging line involves them. A real frustration in this situation is the way the long delay for meetings and input from operations doesn't always give me sufficient feedback to really be able to see how I'm doing. This gets to be so discouraging I find myself falling into the trap of working on less important tasks that I can finish quickly because I need the gratification of seeing things get done.

"Since I come in at 7:30 and stay till 6:00 P.M., I must have the gratification of feeling I've accomplished something every day. But this is becoming a problem because in letting myself be diverted to smaller jobs I can complete— reviewing sales reports, for instance—I dilute time and energy I should be devoting to my large-scale projects."

If you like immediate gratification:

- Create some structure where there isn't any.

    For Peter we designed limited administrative "office hours" (for example, an hour a day to complete time sheets, expense reports, etc.). These daily one-hour periods allowed him to step back and feel he had reached the finish line on something without interfering with his focus on major long-range undertakings. He was able to say at the end of each day, "These small things needed to be done, and today I accomplished them." Next we selected the top four priorities for Peter to hop between. Using a variation of the Master List designed especially for Hoppers, Peter wrote one major project at the top of each blank column. Beneath each heading, Peter listed all of the related To Do items. This enabled him to see at a glance what needed to be accomplished in all four areas.

4. You like to feel busy.

Dennis, the assistant director of a secretarial school, believes that unless he is always busy he's really doing nothing.

"I guess it's a hang-up," he declared. "But I have to keep going from morning till night. I get to work very early and usually leave after everyone else, and I often have luncheon appointments and a couple of meetings at night. On weekends I do volunteer work.

"This keeps me on the go, which I like. But I have to admit I'm frequently exhausted."

If you like to feel busy—but not exhausted:

- Keep track of your changing energy levels throughout the day.
- Rank your current activities according to the energy required to perform each one fairly well.
    Dennis saw that certain tasks required a lot (5's) either because the tasks were hard or because he disliked them. Some activities required only a little energy because they were easier or more enjoyable.
- Schedule your most demanding work for the time of day when you're best able to handle it.
- Reserve the less demanding items for the periods when you tend to drag.

When You Hop

Sometimes you will find yourself Hopping even if you wouldn't ordinarily call yourself a Hopper. See how

Sample Hopper's To Do List

Develop new packaging line with operations people	Prepare a meeting for distributors and sales representatives	Evaluate two products whose sales are lagging	Launch one new product
Read product literature	Arrange tour of facilities	Obtain sales histories by region	Engage market research firm
Meet with engineers from production department	Make hotel arrangements	Review sales reports	Develop test marketing plan
Prepare presentation of findings for executive staff meeting	Make banquet arrangements	Interview salesmen and distributors	Engage advertising agency
Develop retraining program	Prepare and set up displays	Draft telephone survey	Review advertising and marketing proposals
Do cost/benefit analysis	Prepare sample kits	Call in market research firm	Prepare promotion budget
Visit two existing installations	Get speaker	Meet with market research firm to help write survey	Develop materials for distribution to sales force
	Prepare handout materials	Compile product budgets	Confirm production schedules with production department
		Attend focus group sessions	Prepare press releases
		Update competitive analysis	Review media contracts
		Prepare recommendations to top management	Prepare schedule for release
		Assess inventories	
		Develop strategies	

much you see of yourself in the following. Chances are good you'll identify with Bob, Mel, Gil, or Jane.

1. You're bored.

Bob, a graying sales representative for a West Coast beverage firm, started in sales right after college. But his years on the road are taking their toll, and he feels it is time for him to move up to regional manager. Every time an opening comes up, Bob applies for the job, but somebody younger is always chosen for the post. Bob believes he has no future in his present firm. But at forty-eight, he's hesitant to give up his fairly lucrative job for the unknown somewhere else. His discontent has turned into boredom, so to counteract it he Hops in an almost casual way from one call to another and gives little thought to planning his days in the way he formerly did.

If you're bored:

- Address the question of whether you should remain in your present situation.
- While you're deciding whether to investigate other opportunities (1) make a reasonable daily plan, (2) try to stick to it, and (3) reward yourself in some way for making and maintaining the plan.
- Relax and do some pleasant things such as reading or walking so your attitude and energy will improve.

2. You're frustrated.

Mel, the busy operations manager of a small bottled-water company, is suddenly faced with dealing with stricter regulations. Among the new laws are rulings that require inventorying hazardous substances as well as additional lab testing for water quality.

Feeling frustrated and behind the eight ball with the added workload plus his regular jobs, Mel finds himself constantly switching from studying the new laws to his day-by-day obligations. On the day I consulted with him, for example, I found him hopping between (1) reading the latest industry bulletin to check on regulations; (2) calling the company's fleet manager to make sure tires have been rotated; (3) writing memos to employees reminding them to conserve energy; and (4) trying to figure out how to incorporate the new laws into training programs for supervisors.

If you're frustrated:

- Recognize that there are only two ways to deal with frustration productively.
  1. Give up trying to work things out.
  2. Solve the problem that's keeping you frustrated.
  In Mel's situation he understandably wanted his people to stay informed on all current regulations so the comapny would be in compliance with federal standards. But he began to realize that he couldn't accomplish this all by himself. His solution wsa to hire a consultant on retainer to explain new regulations, keep him up-to-date, and help him administer training programs.

3. You're anxious.

Gil, a driven personality and the only one in his family to work his way through college, has climbed to the top of the ladder as national parts manager for an automotive corporation. But Gil is so overly anxious about making sure his department runs smoothly and effectively, he constantly leaves his office—and the "Things to Do" on his desk—to check on the people under him to see how they're doing their jobs. Inevitably this checking takes longer than he thought it would, so by the time Gil returns to his desk his anxiety level—and his "Things to Do"—have expanded to larger proportions.

If you're anxious:

- Devise ways to reduce your anxiety level.
  Anxiety, like frustration, is unavoidable at times.

But it too can be handled in a positive manner through management techniques such as exercise, relaxation therapy, biofeedback, meditation, and healthy eating habits. These approaches can help you cope better with stress in general and minimize its negative effects on your body. Gil learned this when he began closing his door for twenty minutes every morning to relax and practice rhythmic breathing.

- Another way to deal with the uneasiness you experience when you worry about something is to give yourself specific tasks designed to make you feel in control.

  Gil needed to be on top of what was going on in his department—but in a more organized fashion. We found that if he kept a list of his people's current projects and then set aside the last hour of every day to touch base with them, he was able to stay comfortably informed about their progress.

4. You accept too many unnecessary interruptions, phone calls, and drop-in visitors.

Many Hoppers create problems for themselves when they accept too many interruptions, since interruptions are one of our biggest time wasters. In fact, researchers in the time-management field have observed that unless executives protect themselves, they're interrupted approximately every eight minutes.

Take the case of Jane, a thirty-year-old interior designer who looks like a model on a cover of *Vogue*. She was recently promoted to the head designer's job in a fine home-furnishings store, and since she has always been ambitious this is a milestone. But now she is stymied in keeping up with her schedule because of a series of interruptions, phone calls, and drop-in visitors that punctuate her day.

"If it's not a sales representative knocking on my door, it's someone from the store staff or a client on the phone who wants to confer with me," she says. "All of this breaks up my day and takes up all of my time."

If you automatically accept interruptions:

- Consider whether acceptance is the appropriate response at the moment you're interrupted.
- Use a triggering device to help you decide whether the interruptions should be handled immediately, deferred to a later time, or delegated to someone else.

   For Jane, the device was a little sign lettered in red that said "WAIT A MINUTE," taped to the back of a paperweight. The bright red color always drew her gaze and reminded her to stop and think, "What is the best use of my time right now?"
- Learn to say, "I'm sorry, I'm tied up right now," when your top priorities are interrupted.

Rx for Interruptions, Telephone Calls, and Drop-in Visitors

In addition to the suggestions I gave Jane, the following pointers will help you minimize unplanned interruptions, unnecessary phone calls, and unwelcome drop-in visitors.

Interruptions.

Interruptions have many forms, and certainly some don't qualify as time wasters because they're personal or business obligations. For example, if you're someone's assistant on the job, you're paid to be interrupted when your boss needs something from you. Similarly, if you run a business from a home office, your morning of bookkeeping may well be interrupted if a child comes home from school sick. Other interruptions, however, can be delegated, deferred, or even eliminated. Here are more ways to protect yourself:

1. Schedule some quiet time for yourself in which you accept no visitors or phone calls except for real emergencies.
2. When you really need to concentrate:
   • Close your door and put a "DO NOT DISTURB" sign on it.
   • Come to your job early or stay late.
   • Seek refuge in an unused office or space in your company.
   • Take a day off to work at home.
   • Drive your car to a peaceful spot.
   • Rent another office (or motel/hotel room) as your private hideaway.
3. Jot down a short note when you are interrupted to remind you where you broke off. Then you can quickly get back on track when the interruption is finished.

An Interruption Log (an abbreviated version of the Time Log) will make it easy for you to see the nature and pattern of your interruptions. (See sample log and instructions on page 57. This log was filled out by Stephanie, the CEO of an office-support services center that handles word processing, printing, and direct mail.)

The Telephone

Have you ever asked yourself, "Why did I let lengthy phone calls ruin my morning schedule instead of telling people I would have to call them back?" Unless you're superhuman, you probably ask that daily as you switch from the job you are doing to answer the telephone.

Admittedly, the phone (sometimes called the greatest nuisance among conveniences and the greatest convenience among nuisances) is vital to our lives. But it is also a time waster when we permit it to interrupt us regardless of what we're doing. Here are techniques that will help you limit its time-wasting aspects.

1. Cut down on incoming calls that you would normally answer.

Date: February 4

Sample Interruption Log

Person	Issues	Time In	Time Out	Total Time	Did*	Should Have Done
Larraby's (Prospective client)	Wanted quote on price and time frame on project	9:15	9:20	5 mins.	1	3
Theresa Land (Client)	Wanted time for drop off of completed job	10:00	10:03	3 mins.	3	3
Jim (Accountant)	Wanted some numbers	10:15	10:25	10 mins.	2	2
Morris Rogers (Client)	Needs rush job completed today	11:00	11:30	30 mins.	1	1
Caroline (Employee)	Needed help with special requirements on computer	11:45	12:00	15 mins.	1	1
National Securities (Client)	Label info. they gave us was incorrect. Need to re-run labels & affix to brochures	2:00	3:00	60 mins	1 & 3	3
Mark (Employee)	Computer broke down. Need to call service and re-arrange work schedules	3:15	4:00	45 mins.	1	1

*Handled = 1   Deferred = 2   Delegated = 3

- Eliminate them by unplugging the phone, taking it off the hook, or removing yourself to a place where there is no phone.
- Ask someone to screen calls for you. (If you don't have a secretary, people in the office or at home can take turns answering the phone for specified times every day.)
- Use an answering machine.
- Employ an answering service.
- Encourage people who always call *you* to ask for persons on your staff who are equally qualified to help them.

2. • Make good use of secretaries or assistants. Give your support staff these three constantly updated lists of people:
- Persons they should always put through
- Persons they should always put through except during meetings or quiet times.
- Persons you don't want put through to you, but whom you might call back.

Depending on the situation and caller you may want to instruct your secretary or assistant to say the following:

- "He's busy at the moment. Would you like me to interrupt him?"
- "She's involved in a meeting right now. May she call you back when she is free?"
- "He's away from his desk at the moment."

Incidentally, since you can be "involved in meetings" and "away from your desk" just so much, be sure these responses are varied and given in such a way they don't offend the callers.

3. Keep conversations short. Some people have been known to do this by hanging up on themselves— and pretending they were cut off! But if you're not up to doing that, try this potpourri of one-liners:

- "I'm not able to talk right now, so can I get back to you?"
- "I'm working on a rush project."
- "I have someone in my office."

- "This is a bad time for me to talk."
- "I was just on my way out the door."
- "I'm expecting a long-distance call any minute."
- "Someone is waiting here to see me."
- "I can't talk much longer."
- "Is there anything else we need to talk about before we hang up?"
- "It has been great talking to you, but I have to go now."
- "If that winds things up, I must get moving."
- "Someone's at the door."

4. Handle outgoing calls more efficiently. Your outgoing calls can spare you some of the incoming ones. To save time when you make them:
   - Group them together for a specific call/callback period.
   - Place them in priority order.
   - Make sure that calling is the most effective step—should written material be sent first?
   - Have a clear idea of what you want to say and keep all material relevant to the call handy.
   - Determine how you'll handle being put on hold. Will you hang up or do routine paperwork while you wait?
   - When the person you're calling is out, leave a precise message stating who you are and why you called. Let the person who anwers the phone know when you will be available for a return call or ask when is the best time to call back.
   - When you have trouble getting hold of someone, telephone before or after hours. Many busy people often come in early or stay late.
   - Always ask, "Is this a convenient time for you to talk?" If it is, start right in with "The reason I am calling you is . . ."
   - Time-limit your calls.
   - Communicate with people via memos or notes when they're the type who tie you up on the phone.

5. Utilize updated technology. These days it's easy to

save time with these helpful phone features:
- cordless phones
- automatic redial
- speaker phones
- speed dialing
- call waiting
- call forwarding
- built-in timer
- conference calling
- car phones

Drop-Ins:

There are also ways to cut down the interruptions that drop-in visitors cause. Often this challenge is greater than getting off the phone because the person is standing right in front of you. But since drop-ins may have no respect for the value of your time, you have to let them know when you're available and when you're not.

Andrew, a comptroller for a manufacturing firm, has no fixed hours for this and will see a drop-in at any time. His rationale for doing this, and even encouraging it, stems from his Hopping style of accepting interruptions and jumping from task to task. He is convinced that he needs to maintain an open-door policy so he can be instantly alerted if a problem or question comes up, no matter how small it is. But this takes time from Andrew's other work—and more than once he has fallen behind on something critical.

Granted, it's not always easy to determine in advance whether drop-ins really need to see you, whether you need to see them, or whether they just want to talk to you when they have nothing else to do. As with telephone calls, have them screened first. But if that's not possible, you can keep from going overboard like Andrew by doing the following:

- Establish specific open-door periods in which you are available to see people, and make sure people know you have fixed hours for this.

- Have your secretary or assistant schedule appointments.
- Try to intercept oncoming drop-ins outside your office.
- Keep a phone, pencil, or paper in your hand as a sign that you have to get right back to work.
- Don't have additional chairs in your office or, if you must, see that they're occupied by a stack of papers.
- Let people know they've come at a bad time, and ask if someone else can help them or if the visit can wait till later in the day.
- Set time limits at the start by saying you have only five minutes to talk at the moment. If that isn't sufficient, suggest that drop-ins set up an appointment for when you'll have more time.
- Bring the visit to a close with a phrase such as "Before we finish . . ." If drop-ins don't take that hint, (1) remain quiet so the conversation will end; (2) pick up your phone and tell your secretary you'll be with her in a minute; or (3) think of something you need in the vicinity of the drop-in's office and begin slowly walking him or her back while the person is still talking.

As a last resort, you can post this sign on your door for people who constantly interrupt you for insignificant matters: "IF YOU'RE SURE IT'S AN EMERGENCY—COME ON IN."

How You Can Make a Tendency to Hop Work for You

Hopping can work in two ways: in a positive manner that works for you or in a negative manner that holds you back. When Hopping works in a negative way you (1) may leave important tasks unfinished, (2) feel confused or anxious, (3) lose track of time or valuable items, or (4) find other people have difficulty working with you.

On the other hand, when Hopping works in a positive way you can (1) accomplish several major achievements at once, (2) make good use of your changing energy levels during the day, and (3) stay alert and motivated by moving from one activity to another.

Gail, a divorcée with small children to support, has learned to be a Hopper in a highly positive way. After taking many real-estate courses and exams and working extensively in the field, she now heads a real-estate corporation and specializes in selling townhouses and country condominiums. She puts in ten-hour workdays, but in between business commitments and taking care of her children and home, she studies singing seriously and sings in a small opera company. She also swims on a daily basis or rides an exercise bike twenty minutes a day. She's a perfect example of a positive Hopper because she moves successfully from one thing to another.

Instant Summary for a Hopper

Knowing where you're going to land next and planning your leaps and jumps to get there is all that separates the successful Hopper from the unsuccessful one. Hopping works well only when you are comfortable and in control. If you begin to feel like a hamster on an exercise wheel, running faster and faster but not getting anywhere, remind yourself to:

1. Slow down for a minute.
2. Eliminate as many distractions and interruptions as possible. Close your door and take your phone off the hook for a while.
3. Create some structure in your day by selecting a few high-priority tasks to do during your highest energy level.
4. Concentrate your efforts for whatever time period you can manage. Break projects down into mini-goals and move ahead one step at a time.

5. Use a timer or other mechanisms to remind yourself to keep on schedule.
6. Try to deal with frustration, anxiety, or boredom in a positive, productive manner.
7. Take time to relax and reward yourself along the way.

CHAPTER 5

Perfectionist Plus

*I never seem to have time to do all the things
I want to do as well as I believe they should
be done.*

In the real world there isn't always time to aspire to perfection in all the things you need, or want, to do. When you try to do everything at the highest possible standard there are many activities that you never get to. At the end of a day you feel burned out because you have "failed" to be perfect in every undertaking. You also face the constant danger that in trying to excel at everything, you end up doing nothing well and are often forced by deadline pressure to do a critically important task less thoroughly than you should.

A Perfectionist Plus, however, has a difficult time acknowledging that his or her compulsively high standards are unrealistic and that doing *everything* perfectly isn't necessary for every task. To find out if this is one of your styles, take the following quiz.

Are You a Perfectionist Plus?

As you answer Never (N), Occasionally (O), or Frequently (F), rate yourself according to the following scale.

Never	Occasionally	Frequently
0 points	1 point	2 points

N   O   F

1. Few things bother me more than working with a person who is disorganized.
2. I rewrite letters and reports a number of times to get them just right.
3. I get so involved with details I often can't complete projects on time.
4. When making a presentation, I feel it's essential to mention every detail to support a point.
5. I feel frustrated when I don't get to every item on my To Do List.
6. I rarely skim when I read because I'd hate to overlook any critical details or nuances.
7. After completing a job, I'm seldom really satisfied with the results.
8. I work a lot of overtime to complete things I can't accomplish during normal working hours.
9. I become upset when people don't maintain the schedule we establish.
10. When I assign work to someone, I like to map out precisely what is expected and specify frequent checkpoints so I can be sure the person is handling the assignment as I would.

Totals:

0–6 points	You're not really a Perfectionist Plus.
7–13 points	You have strong Perfectionist Plus tendencies.
14–20 points	You're a full-fledged Perfectionist Plus.

Why People Have a Perfectionist-Plus Style

1. They have a hard time distinguishing between high standards and superhuman expectations.

Perfectionist-Plus individuals, who compulsively set high standards for themselves and fail to recognize how unrealistic their expectations are, believe their standards are perfectly normal and commonplace. Because of this they become discouraged, never realizing that what is below average to them is often perfectly acceptable to others. They never think to ask themselves, "*Who* is setting these high standards?" or "Who else is keeping tabs?"

To keep from living at odds with themselves in their pursuit of perfection, they'd do well to recognize that even if other people are interested in their achievements, those people are judging them with an entirely different set of expectations and objectives. Moreover, they need to accept that when they lower their expectations, they are not giving up all standards and settling for second-rate living.

The latter is Larry's problem as he struggles with his high standards not only in his working life but in his personal life too. At thirty-five he's on his way up as an investment banker and vice-president of a Fortune 500 firm. His work demands long hours but at home he's interested in a great many things (which he wants to do perfectly, of course): besides remodeling a weekend home, he also fits in hobbies that include sailing, cross-country skiing, swimming, tennis, and raising tropical fish. The day we discussed his hobbies, he was thinking of adding photography as well because a colleague at the investment house wanted him to join his photography club. "I ought to be able to handle it," Larry said. "But sometimes I feel that I don't get the pleasure from my hobbies that I should because I'm too busy worrying whether I'm buying the right equipment and doing things the right way."

If you have difficulty distinguishing between high standards and superhuman expectations:

- Begin by looking at the bottom line. Compare your assumption of what's required to the reality of the situation.
- Learn to say no.

  Perfectionist-Plus people tend to say yes to requests for their time more often than they should for a variety of reasons:

  1. They don't want to let people down.
  2. They're afraid they won't be asked again.
  3. They fear they won't be liked.
  4. They feel obligated—or they really have a desire to help.

  But if you always say yes, not only will you have no time to take care of your own needs, you'll ultimately disappoint the people you're trying to accommodate because you won't have sufficient energy or hours to carry through on your promises.

- Follow these steps the next time you feel tempted to say yes when you want to say no:

  1. Remind yourself of your priorities. You do not have unlimited time and resources, so consider what other activity will not get done if you say yes to this one. Is the trade-off worth it?
  2. Realize that you can say no firmly but pleasantly. Express your regrets and offer a reason if you choose to.

     "I'm sorry, but I have to say no."

     "I don't like to disappoint you, but I must say no."

     "I'll have to say no because of a prior commitment."

     "I need to say no because I'm already overloaded and not in a position to take anything else on right now."

     "I'm going to say no because I couldn't do justice to what you're asking me to do while these other things are still hanging."

3. Remember, no one will respect your time if you don't. Asserting yourself is healthy when it allows you to strike a balance between your own needs and the needs of others.

In Larry's case, I suggested he do three things:

1. Display prominent "WAIT A MINUTE" signs in both his office and home to encourage him to stop and consider whether or not to take on another activity.
2. Evaluate whether adding photography to his hobbies and joining a club was currently the best use of his time.
3. Tell his business colleague (assuming he decided against photography for the time being), "I'm going to have to say no to joining your club right now, but I know I'd enjoy photography so I'd like to take a raincheck for when I have fewer commitments."

2. They're trying to please someone in their past.

Many of the perfectionists I counsel are trying to live up to the expectations of a teacher, parent, or other authority figure who wanted them to be accomplished and outstanding. Since they were rewarded as children for superior performance, as adults they think that the only way to deserve a reward is to do everything perfectly.

Most of the time these Perfectionist-Plus people who associate being perfect with being accepted and liked are overly dependent on external rewards and pats on the back to keep going. They become so others-centered they lose sight of their priorities, and the shadow of the people who expect much from them is always looking over their shoulder.

Barbara, with a high-pressured executive job in an advertising firm, is still trying in her mid-thirties to live up to her mother's expectations. "My mother always encouraged me to have high aspirations," she said, "and she told me I could do anything if I made up my mind to do it. As a result, my biggest dream was having a great career. But I also wanted a husband and children, and a big rambling house in the country."

Today Barbara has achieved all these things. But she's pulled in so many directions, her life is one big loose end. She married as soon as she finished college, then cut her two-week honeymoon short to take a job with an advertising agency as a junior copywriter. "My mother was ecstatic," she told me. "She was pleased to death with my start."

Barbara's first son and a big promotion came eleven months later, with Barbara working till early afternoon on the day the baby was delivered. Her second year out of college brought a second child—and a second big promotion. Within five years Barbara had progressed to an account executive's spot.

By then she and her sales-manager husband were able to put their incomes together and buy a house in the country. But they needed both of their salaries to renovate the run-down house and pay for live-in help because of their early commute to the city and their late return at night. Eventually Barbara became a senior account executive. But this job took her on the road most of the week. Things piled up in her office and home, and even though her mother was pleased at Barbara's "perfect" life, the dream Barbara had as a child was a nightmare as an adult. "Nothing is ever as perfect as I want it to be," she sighed. "I feel I have little time for my sons, and, frankly, I'm so snowed under I don't know which way to turn."

If you're a Perfectionist Plus, evaluate whether you are doing what you truly want or are just trying to please someone in your past:

- Learn to challenge your assumption that in order to feel valued by others and yourself, you have to drive yourself to achieve perfection. Ask yourself:
  1. What's the payoff in this for me?

2. How am I letting other people's expectations control the way I am living?
3. Do I spend a lot of time worrying about what my boss thinks of my performance?
4. Do I feel as though I won't be noticed unless my work is exceptional?
5. Am I afraid of being fired for making a mistake?
6. Can I be objective about the quality of my work, or do I depend on feedback from others to tell me how I'm doing?

When Barbara answered these questions, the first thing she realized was that she'd never stopped before to think about *what* she was doing or *why* she was doing it. She had achieved so much so quickly that she needed every ounce of energy just to keep up—never mind standing back and evaluating the results.

Once she thought about this, she soon recognized that even though everyone else seemed pleased with her success, she was now miserable. "I'd once thought it would be enough if I just made everyone happy," she said. "But what good is it if they're all happy and I'm not? Why keep trying to do everything perfectly if I'm beginning to hate what I'm doing?"

This evaluation was a major first step in helping Barbara refocus her efforts. She learned that she really did enjoy working at the agency. But the constant travel required of her was causing her to feel out of control. Once she made this evaluation, she decided to transfer into a lower-profile administrative position within the company that didn't involve travel. She took a cut in salary—and, with her lower-profile position, her mother can't boast about her in the way she previously did.

But Barbara feels that the extra time she now has for her children more than compensates.

3. They believe they should be able to do everything themselves and do it all well.

Many perfectionists are afraid to delegate because (1) they think they'll appear inadequate if they don't take full responsibility for everything themselves; and (2) they believe other people won't do a job their way. How often have you ended a day when you tried to do everything on your own with the frustrated feeling: "I didn't accomplish a thing all day!"

More than likely you did make some progress, and you probably did something fairly well. But because you drove yourself to perfection you felt discouraged when your day's achievements matched neither your perfectionist's standards nor the timetable you set for completing a task.

Cheryl is a supervisor in the employee-benefits department of a large corporation, and she's so afraid her department won't function perfectly, she insists on overseeing everything herself. She's long on Perfectionist-Plus details but short on managerial skills, so in order to become a better manager and rise on the corporate ladder she's going to school in the evening to get her M.B.A.

Despite her work and night school, however, she wants her home to be perfect, too. The light switches are smudge-free, and her husband and children leave the house color-coordinated every morning. "You wouldn't believe what they'd put on if I didn't get their clothes out," she says wearily.

If you believe you should be able to do everything yourself:

- Learn to delegate before you become so overwhelmed you're dangerously close to burn-out.

    When Perfectionist-Plus people don't learn to delegate, it eventually becomes impossible for them to take on new, more interesting responsibilities because there's literally no time left in the day. And at that point, no one can help out because no one has been taught how.
- Before you reach that point, answer these questions to see if you're giving yourself and your subordi-

nates the necessary opportunities to grow and develop:

1. Can someone else adequately do this work for me:
   • Faster than I can?
   • With more attention than I can manage now?
   • At a lower hourly rate than the cost of my time?
2. Will delegating this work give my people an opportunity for professional growth?
3. Will delegating this work give me an opportunity to concentrate on the longer-range planning and projects that only I can do?

If you answered yes to any of the above, follow the next six steps to delegate the work effectively:

1. Define the exact nature of the work.
2. Select the appropriate person to whom the assignment will be given.
3. Clearly describe all aspects of the assignment, including desired results, time frames, and nature of progress reports (if any).
4. Ask for feedback so you will know:
   • If the delegate is willing and/or able to undertake the assignment.
   • If the delegate understands your instructions.
5. Give support and direction as needed.
6. Review and evaluate results.

I suggested that Cheryl begin by letting people on her staff develop the rough drafts of pension plans instead of keeping on top of everything herself during the early stages. I advised her to get started on this by calling a meeting with her assistants to discuss how everyone could help one another do the total job better. To Cheryl's surprise, she discovered that though she'd always thought she was giving her staff plenty of tasks, they actually welcomed more work. Gradually she learned to delegate, and as a result she had more hours to do more of the tasks that she enjoyed and that only she could do.

At home she started to delegate, too, and she found that when she showed she expected her family to do their share of the chores, they did pitch in and help.

When People Have a Perfectionist-Plus Style

At certain times everyone is more likely to adopt a Perfectionist-Plus style, such as when you're nervous about the outcome of a project.

June is a project administrator for a government agency that helps teenagers from low-income families gain job experience and training. She has been in the job for the past ten years and still agonizes over every detail. One of her major responsibilities is recommending new projects and getting the funds to implement them. But June is always afraid that her staff and the other bureau people involved will not complete the various pieces of the grant in the shape she wants them and by the date she wants them. Consequently she procrastinates getting the whole project underway by concentrating on minor preliminary tasks and unnecessary discussion of other issues. She uses her perfectionistic approach as a strategy to avoid the more important task.

If you avoid important jobs because you're nervous about the outcome:

- Try to overcome the fear by planning out the worst-case scenario.

  When working with June, I suggested that she imagine the most horrifying things that her people could do to her in the process of putting the grant together. Her greatest fear was that she would come in the day of the final deadline and find out that the entire group had quit without turning in their assignments. But in her ten years on the job the "worst" has never happened, and it's quite unlikely that it will. There had been some close calls at deadline times, but June recognized that by building in extra time cushions and forcing herself to initiate each project without delay instead of wasting time on low-priority activities, she could control her nervousness and not slip into a paralysis of perfectionism.

In another situation Marshall, a partner in a chain of Florida shoe stores, is apprehensive about initiating a computerized billing system. Although the new system could save the firm much time and paperwork, Marshall fears his partner and he may lose money if everything doesn't work out. He has already spent endless hours perfecting the manual system they use, and now as he works and reworks all details related to the acquisition of the new system, he has practically lost all sight of its goal.

Marshall needs to understand that the time he's spending worrying about the prospective system may eventually result in missed deadlines on other important projects. In fact, the latter happens frequently, much to Marshall's despair, because Perfectionist-Plus individuals, with their all-or-nothing approach about every little detail, usually don't accomplish even one-third of what they've put on their To Do List.

If, like Marshall, you have this problem:

• Look at the profitability factor of each of the items on your To Do List.

Obviously the new billing system is important to Marshall and should be handled carefully. But other critical items on his To Do List need attention also. Since there will never be enough hours in the day to achieve perfection in every endeavor, Marshall and other Perfectionist-Plus people must first concentrate on those items with the biggest payoff, or profitability factor, and budget their time accordingly. In this way nothing major will get squeezed out in the time crunch.

Once the profitability factor is accounted for, Perfectionist-Plus individuals should think about how much they might enjoy doing each task. Unfortunately, their noses are so close to the grindstone they often don't see that there are other pleasures (besides completing things in perfect order) to be gained from their work. For instance, Marshall liked to go along in the trucks that made drop-offs to the various stores. He felt that gave him a different perspective from which to view the chain's operations, and he also simply enjoyed getting out of his office.

The Perfectionist-Plus To Do List takes into account profitability, enjoyability, and the necessity of delegating some task. It encourages Marshall and his Perfectionist-Plus counterparts to (1) get the most important things done, (2) concentrate on what they enjoy, and (3) allow other employees to get essential additional experience. (See below for Instructions for the Perfectionist-Plus To Do List and page 77 for Marshall's sample list.)

Instructions for Perfectionist-Plus To Do List

1. List items you want to be taken care of.
2. On a scale of 1 (High) to 5 (Low), put down the number that indicates how profitable it will be to have that task performed (i.e., will it be a good use of your time or someone else's time to take care of that item at this point?).
3. Using the same scale, put down the number that indicates how enjoyable to you personally the task will be.
4. Add A and B together.
5. The lower the score, the higher priority ranking that To Do item commands. Put your listed items in ranked order.
6. Can any of the items be delegated to someone else to take care of? If so, indicate them with a check mark.
7. You now have a completed To Do List, telling you

which tasks you will perform, in what order, and which tasks can be delegated to others. The idea behind this is that you maintain a balance between various factors, so you don't burn out trying to do it all well.

8. Feel free to move around items as needed on your final list. Items with high profitability/low enjoyment will need to come ahead of those with high enjoyment/low profitability most of the time. But at least you can see the basis on which you're making your choice.

How You Can Make a Perfectionist-Plus Style Work for You

There's nothing wrong with a Perfectionist-Plus style when, in a positive way, you work within your Perfectionist-Plus framework to (1) identify high-priority activities in which results are sufficiently important to justify top standards, (2) focus on those tasks, and (3) strive for excellence in them. Only when perfectionism becomes a mania does it hinder your effectiveness and become a poor use of your time.

In certain situations perfectionism is a necessity. Take Ted, who's employed as a geophysicist in the natural-gas industry. He applies the principles of physics, geology, mathematics, chemistry, and engineering to the study of the earth, and his dedication to perfectionism has put him in the forefront of researchers in his field. He *has* to be a Perfectionist Plus because of the extreme detail called for in his work and its eventual impact on major decision-making.

For Ted—in the detailed nature of his work—striving for perfection makes sense. But for many people—and for many jobs—it makes equally good sense to put perfection in its place by telling yourself it's all right if less

Sample Perfectionist-Plus To Do List

Item	A = Profitability	B = Enjoyability	Score (A + B)	Rank	Can be Delegated
Visit store #1 to see how sale shoes are set up on display rack	5	3	8	8	
Talk to Doug in store #2 about his plans for back-to-school display	5	3	8	7	
Get Lee's input for back-to-school promotions	1	2	3	2	
Check stock in store #3	2	4	6	6	
Cancel plans for Wed. photography course	5	5	10	10	✓ (Sharon)
Discuss computerized billing system with Lee	2	3	5	4	
See if Brent has moved new shipment in warehouse	5	3	8	9	
Make drop-off to store #3	3	2	5	5	✓ (Brent)
See if Lee ordered correct number of Nikes	1	3	4	3	
Go over July invoices with Sharon	1	1	2	1	

significant tasks leave your hands in less than perfect order.

You can accomplish this by creating self-imposed deadlines for the low-payoff items and determining, within that time frame, what's the *least* work you can do to end up with an acceptable product.

When you do this and cut down on feeling you have to be perfect in everything, you'll experience a new sense of freedom. By the same token, as you realize that from mistakes you learn lessons for improving, you'll become less hard on yourself and the people with whom you work. Slowly and surely you'll find out you don't always have to dot every *i* and cross every *t*

Instant Summary for Perfectionist Plus

If you're a Perfectionist Plus, you have difficulty acknowledging that your high expectations of yourself may be unrealistic or unnecessary. Although you'll probably never accept the idea that *all* of your standards should be lowered, you can learn to identify the 20 percent that deserve your utmost efforts—and then try the following:

1. Look first at the bottom line. Compare your assumption of what's required to the reality of the situation. Realize that your standards may be unnecessarily high.
2. Ask yourself if you're still attempting to please someone in your past. If so, is the effort worth it?
3. Say no to new activities that may overload your plate.
4. Identify the high-priority activities in which results are sufficiently important to justify top standards. Give less attention and effort to activities with a lower priority.
5. Learn to delegate effectively. Reserve for yourself those activities that you enjoy and those that only you can do.
6. If you're afraid of turning out less than perfect

work, imagine the worst that could happen if you did. Is it really that awful? Could you handle it?

7. Take time to relax and reward yourself along the way.

CHAPTER 6

Allergic to Detail

I'm impatient with project follow-through because I just can't be bothered with all the little details.

Allergic-to-Detail people thrive on working and living in the eye of the hurricane. They're bold individuals who enjoy dealing with challenging projects and engaging in many activities at once. But in their rush to get moving, it seems as though they expect other people to read their minds: they tend to overlook all kinds of essential details. For example, a builder involved in a major project neglects to tell his construction-site crew which way the doors should face. A publicist enthralled with the sit-down dinner she's planning for her staff makes lavish preparations, but never investigates whether or not she has enough chairs for her guests. Generally people such as these aren't really aware of the results of their style till somebody mentions it.

Are You Allergic to Detail?

To find out, take the following quiz. As you answer Never (N), Occasionally (O), or Frequently (F), rate yourself according to the following scale.

Never	Occasionally	Frequently
0 points	1 point	2 points

1. I'd much rather formulate a plan than carry it out.
2. When I assign a project to someone, I generally describe the desired outcome of the project and then leave the execution to someone else.
3. I usually can't be bothered with tidying up my desk.
4. I don't like to take the time to review detailed numerical analyses.
5. I always seem to be in a rush and leave something important behind when I leave the house.
6. I write memos only when I can't deliver a message in person or by phone.
7. I forget birthdays, anniversaries, meetings, and appointments.
8. I give my assistant free rein to screen my mail and handle routine correspondence.
9. I get impatient with people who feel compelled to tell me every little detail about something.
10. When reading my mail or business periodicals, I quickly scan items of interest and toss the rest.

Totals:

0–6 points	You're not really an Allergic to Detail.
7–13 points	You have strong Allergic to Detail tendencies.
14–20 points	You're a full-fledged Allergic to Detail.

Why People Have an Allergic-to-Detail Style

1. They enjoy dealing with the broad picture.

Most people who are Allergic to Detail see themselves as flexible, well-rounded persons with a variety of interests. As they pursue these interests they enjoy making all the big decisions. But once those big decisions are made, they like to move on to something else and let others take care of the more routine details.

Stewart, the catering manager at a highly successful restaurant, was convinced the owners should expand by adding to their current on-premise facilities an off-premise catering service. "We're ready to make a decision," the two owners said to him, "if you can really sell us with a budget and presentation."

With that as his encouragement, Stewart spent many hours on a presentation and budget. He depended on his fairly new secretary to pull the right folders from his files, and he used the material she brought him as the basis for his recommendations.

The material he found in his current files was exactly what he wanted to push. But as he got excited over that and hurriedly wrote the presentation so he could move on to other tasks (such as devising some new menu items and arranging corporate functions), Stewart overlooked the important detail of checking through his predecessor's files too. Not until the day the presentation was due did he think of telling his secretary to look through those files. To his consternation, he found substantial amounts of material from previous experiments that contradicted a number of his conclusions. Stewart had to revamp his entire presentation to prevent the loss of thousands of dollars budgeted for projects that would not succeed.

If you enjoy dealing with the broad picture:

- Make sure you're looking at the *whole* picture. This means carefully laying out a plan of operation.

Stewart only took a quick look around, and then plunged into writing the presentation without bothering to check whether certain of his assumptions were correct, such as:

1. His secretary had enough experience to pull all of the right folders.
2. She only needed to check the current files.

Stewart was lucky this time. But not taking the time to plan carefully up front could have cost him his job.

2. They're too impatient to handle follow-up.

The impatience for which Allergic to Details are famous may be partly rebellion against constraints they felt in the past. But whatever the reason, this impatience, coupled with the excitement of coming up with ideas and initiating new projects, makes Allergic-to-Detail individuals weak on follow-through. As a result, crucial items often fall through the cracks.

Lee, Marshall's partner in the Florida shoe store chain, is constantly missing key elements in his hurried quest for short-term results. Because he never takes the time to organize his order copies, he either overbuys or forgets to order stock. As a result, he does such things as placing an order for twenty pairs of shoes and—when only ten come in—immediately ordering ten more pairs because he fails to remember that ten more are still due. Thus when the second half of the first order arrives—plus his order for the additional ten—he winds up with ten pairs he didn't need, therefore lowering his profit margin.

Lee also fails to get shipments out to various stores on time. With his habit of recording sales records on loose scraps of paper, he often forgets to round them up in time for the monthly billing.

If you're impatient with follow-up:

- Get someone to say "stop" and force you to at least *see* what's involved in follow-up procedures.

- Arrange for follow-up procedures by making sure your To Do List clearly indicates who will do this.

As a start toward helping him manage more effectively, I suggested that Lee write down what he wanted to do on a simple Allergic-to-Detail's To Do List that contains only two columns: What To Do and Who Will Do It. (See page 85.)

3. They like to move quickly and therefore resist routine tasks.

Many Allergic to Details are quick thinkers with boundless energy. They rely on their intuition for their good ideas, and often they're innovative entrepreneurs who are willing to take risks. They're anything but lazy. As they juggle many balls in the air, though, they continually say they really dislike the routine managing phase of their enterprise.

"I see the job and I sell the job, but then I've got to run the job, too?" asks Marilyn, who, along with being president and operator of a contracting firm, is pursuing her M.B.A., teaching a course on entrepreneurship, lecturing extensively on women in business, and developing a professional comedy act.

She hates details with a passion. When she came to me, she had just completed a $10,000 contracting job and was unable to remember where she put the check. On that same day she missed an appointment for an estimate, scheduled two painting jobs at identical times, and forgot to order special brushes her crew needed for a job. She was also beginning to alienate customers because she didn't make the time to return their phone calls.

"I'm terrible with the little stuff," she admitted, "and because I like to work quickly and not be stuck in one place, it's hard for me to settle down to working on administrative tasks."

Sample Allergic-to-Detail To Do List

What to Do	Who Will Do It
1. Fix up showcase windows in each location	The managers or, if I want it done correctly, I will do it
2. Restock Nikes and Adidas in the stores	Only me
3. Fire an incompetent employee	Hopefully my partner. If not, I will
4. Obtain weekly work hours from each store manager	Me
5. Pay bills	My partner
6. Order lumber and wall material for the new store	My partner
7. Empty out my office trash can	My partner
8. Go to the lawyer re: partnership agreement	Both of us
9. Buy shoes from the Reebok salesman at 1:00	Me
10. Go to display company and pick up some sale tickets for the window	My partner
11. Take salesman out to lunch on Tuesday	Both of us
12. Drop off tax deposit at the bank	Either one of us

If you like to move quickly and resist handling routine tasks:

- Create simple paperwork systems to organize the information you need to keep track of.

To help Marilyn, I first designed clear, easy-to-follow production sheets that contained spaces to check off each piece of equipment as she loaded items onto her truck. In this way neither Marilyn nor her crew members needed to rely on memory to account for all their items when they started or finished a job. We also created estimate sheets and devised a filing system with a minimal number of easy-to-spot, color-coded action folders. In Marilyn's case we used green for financial matters and red for urgent items since those two areas caused her the greatest trouble.

The number of tasks Marilyn had taken on compared to the hours she had to complete them was another trouble spot, so I had her write up a task list and estimate the amount of time each task took. The total, to everyone's amazement, came to 587 hours of work a week—and with Marilyn's current management system she was hardly meeting a fifth of her obligations. To improve this ineffective system I suggested she start immediately to use the Allergic-to-Details specialized two-column To Do List. In this way nothing would get buried or forgotten.

• Get Help.

Once we created Marilyn's paperwork system, we arranged for her to engage a part-time secretary to take care of the details and follow-ups she was bound to overlook with her quick-thinking, fast-moving style.

When People Have an Allergic-to-Detail Style

As we have seen, all people whose primary organizational style is Allergic to Detail are particularly susceptible to overlooking items they should note. But even persons who don't have this style can fall into it at certain times—for instance, when they're temporarily overloaded. The following are two common situations.

1. You are responsible for too many aspects of a job.

It's easy to forget details when you must drop what you're doing to rush on to something else. Ellen, a senior editor at a national magazine, is quick to nod in agreement. She loves the challenge of her multifaceted job, but she's pulled in so many directions she doesn't have time to remember every little detail.

"Take yesterday," she pointed out. "I spent the whole day running behind from the moment I got to the office. Before I could sit down, my boss came in with a memo listing at least six different things she wanted me to pursue—and I didn't know what to do first. Because those jobs took so much of my time, a manuscript I wanted to recheck had to be sent to the printer before I could get to it.

"Then late in the day a financial expert with whom I'd scheduled a phone interview for an upcoming story called to say the time we'd set would not work out for him, and the only way he could talk to me would be if I came to his racquet club and interviewed him there. With the taxi situation, I knew it would take me at least an hour to get down to his club. But since I was on a deadline, I had to have his input so I left the office in a rush to catch up with him.

"In my hurry I left some important folders I needed for the interview back on my office desk, so some of the things I wanted to ask never did get asked. And I also forgot to take with me a letter that I had to mail that night."

If you're responsible for too many aspects of a job:

• Go over your priorities so you know what to do first.

A feeling of being pressured leads straight to scattered thinking. The first thing Ellen had to do was to reexamine her daily priorities. When we met we concentrated on this and began to reschedule her time so her energy could be focused on first things first.

By assigning prominent spots to material that was in process or that needed to be grabbed quickly, Ellen could more easily stay on top of what was where. The biggest help was putting a poster on the back of her door that said, "ARE YOU SURE YOU HAVE EVERYTHING?" with a basket next to it for outgoing mail and other items.

2. You have to cover a lot of ground in a short amount of time.

Joel, the owner of a small flower shop, has the long-term goal of owning at least three other shops in adjacent communities. He has given himself a four-year period to expand to this goal. But he is becoming overwhelmed with the activities and details of his present life that he feels will lead to his future:

- Taking college management and entrepreneurship courses.
- Giving increased personal attention to his present flower shop patrons.
- Building customer contacts through participation in local affairs in the communities where he hopes to expand.

"And I'm starting to feel as overwhelmed as the proverbial absentminded professor in my personal life too," he admitted. "I can never find my belongings when I get dressed in the morning, and after work, when I get ready to go to my health club I find I forgot to wash my clothes and organize my equipment. By the time I get things together it's too late to go to the club."

If you have to do a lot in a short time:
- Minimize forgetting by recording a thought.
  Because Joel is in a hurry to do a lot in a relatively short period of time, he understandably has his days of forgetting what he wants or needs to remember. One solution for him is to carry around

a pad of paper (or a small tape recorder) and jot down or record a significant phrase that will jog his memory later on. (One word of advice, though: Joel needs to make sure that the "significant phrase" will still have meaning to him a day or two later!)

• Tack up reminders where you can't miss them.

Joel can also tape reminders on his bathroom mirror, refrigerator door, steering wheel of his car, telephone, and anyplace else that will catch his eye as he dashes past.

• Streamline all procedures.

It's obvious Joel needs his gym bag packed and kept by his office door. But as an added precaution I advised him to also make a list of everything else he needs to take with him as he moves between rushing out to take courses and going to other communities to participate in their affairs. This avoids forgetfulness as well as a last-minute hassle.

Additional Suggestions for Making an Allergic-to-Detail Style More Productive

1. Set up a tickler file in which you have 31 separate folders marked for each day of the month. As things come up that you'll need to do on a certain day of the month, toss them into your folder for that day. In this way you won't lose airline tickets, notices of meetings, or bills that need attention. You can even use your tickler file as a means of remembering important dates such as birthdays, anniversaries, and other special occasions. The tickler file will automatically keep you on top of details if you get in the habit of looking at it every day.

2. Minimize the problems you have finding the belongings you need each day with "progressive dressing." This legitimizes walking in the door and kicking off your shoes, going into the next room and dropping your briefcase, throwing your coat

over the arm of the sofa as you pass, etc. In the morning trace this path in reverse.

If you are racing ahead and forgetting essential details it can't be emphasized enough that you need to say that important word "Stop" several times a day. You'll find that by taking sufficient time for following up and accounting for details (no matter how tiresome it seems) you'll get and feel in control of your life and then be free to be genuinely creative in dealing with the challenging projects and activities Allergic to Details enjoy.

Instant Summary for an Allergic to Detail

Allergic to Details are often found on the fast track, and their energy and enthusiasm can be critical to the success of a new idea. But most new ideas are only as good as their follow-through, so Allergic to Details have to make sure this aspect of development is not neglected. Sometimes setting up systems can seem like a detail in itself to Allergic to Details, but the following guidelines will help.

1. Create simple, basic routines to follow.
2. Minimize the problem of forgetting.
   • Record your thoughts.
   • Tack up reminders where you can't miss them.
   • Keep all materials and equipment handy for the various activities of your day.
3. Find someone to help you devise follow-up procedures and carry them out.
4. Take time to relax and reward yourself along the way.

CHAPTER 7

Fence Sitter

When faced with a number of choices I have trouble making up my mind.

If you constantly seesaw back and forth between saying "Should I" or "Shouldn't I?" chances are good you seldom accomplish all the things you want to do. That's the predicament most Fence Sitters have. They waste their time and energy waiting for every option and objection to be collected. As ideas and choices run through their minds, they become so overwhelmed they don't know where to begin.

For example, on a small scale, a medical technologist who has the choice of attending the opera, a dinner party, or a travel lecture on a Saturday night is so unable to make a choice he ends up staying home watching reruns on television.

On a larger scale, a manager for a greeting-card manufacturer lives comfortably with his wife and son in a restored gatehouse on his parents' property. He has lived there since his marriage, but for the past ten years he has been trying to decide (1) whether to pull up family roots and move to another part of the country; (2) buy a house or a condominium in a nearby town; or (3) stay where he is, where the rent is cheap and his parents can help his family when he is on the road. Neither the manager nor the technologist ever came to a decision. But by following this "no-decision" style they give up opportunities to get on with their lives.

Are You a Fence Sitter?

To find out if Fence Sitting is one of your organizational styles, take the following quiz. As you answer Never (N), Occasionally, (O), or Frequently (F), rate yourself according to the following scale.

Never	Occasionally	Frequently
O points	1 point	2 points

N O F

1. Do you have trouble making decisions?
2. Do you put off making decisions?
3. Do you pressure yourself to make the "perfect" choice?
4. Do you have difficulty ranking your priorities?
5. Do you worry about not having enough information to make a decision?
6. Do you give yourself too many alternatives from which to choose?
7. Do you hold back on decisions because of the risks involved?
8. Do you worry about whether you made the right decision?
9. Do you take so long to make a decision you miss some favorable outcomes?
10. Do you let others make important decisions involving you?

Totals:

0–6 points	You're not really a Fence Sitter.
7–13 points	You have strong Fence-Sitting tendencies.
14–20 points	You're a full-fledged Fence Sitter.

Why People Have a Fence-Sitter Style

1. You don't know what you really want.

Good decisions are possible only when you know what you want and have your priorities in order.

Gabe, the owner of a large New England foundry that casts and machines parts for decorative brass household items, cannot decide whether to move his foundry to the Southwest or stay where he is. He feels pressure to relocate because (1) many of his competitors have done it, (2) the marketplace for his product is growing at a faster rate in the Southwest because of a larger volume of home building, and (3) energy and labor costs are cheaper.

On the other hand, if Gabe leaves he knows he will displace a lot of people, including some senior management persons who have been with him for years. Although some of those managers have agreed to relocate, others definitely prefer to stay where they are.

If you don't know what you want:

- Evaluate your needs, priorities, and desires.

   Gabe decided that the issue at hand was really whether to keep the business competitive or to let it phase itself out. He knew he wasn't ready to retire, but he still didn't relish the idea of starting all over again with new people in the Southwest.

   Since he needed a solution that was somewhere in between, Gabe began to look for a partner who had an established foundry in the Southwest, but who wanted some additional capital and fresh creative input. When he found such a person for a joint venture, he was able to send down his managers who were willing to relocate while he and the remaining management team maintained the New England operation.

2. You're afraid to make the wrong choice.

We almost always feel some anxiety both before and after making a decision. But excess worrying is an unnecessary drain because there is no such thing as a perfect choice or decision. Most decisions are somewhat reversible too, and realistic people know this.

When Dana was made a partner in a Chicago law firm, she felt that although she had never entertained, she wanted to celebrate her promotion by entertaining her partners and their spouses. In the past she had seldom asked people to her home because she was far too busy with work. As a result she was an inexperienced hostess, totally unsure of herself, and she wondered whether to take the risk of throwing a dinner party. She knew it was highly important for the event to go well, but because entertaining was so new to her she worried constantly:

- "Should I mix business and pleasure?"
- "Is a party at home a wise choice, or should I take people out?"
- "Will everybody get along or will some persons clash?"
- "How will I know whether or not people are enjoying themselves?"
- "Will they like the way I do things when they see me in my home?"
- "Should I have a sit-down dinner, or should it be a buffet?"

Actually, most of Dana's worries were in her head, and instead of sitting on the fence about this (almost a month and a half) she needed to get comfortable with the idea that entertaining her colleagues was all right to do. When she finally gave the party, with some assistance from a caterer, it was a great success.

If you're afraid you'll make a wrong choice:

- Realize that there really are no wrong choices—provided your reasons for making the choice are well thought-out.

You can control how you go about making a decision, but you can't control its outcome. You make the best decision you can at the time and what happens, happens. However, the outcome—good or bad—serves as a trial-and-error learning process that will provide you with the informational feedback that's essential for growth and development. The outcome of a choice may not be what you want, or even what you anticipate, but if you don't take the risk you'll never have the opportunity to move on to a new experience.

3. You don't know how to start moving.

Edythe, a fashion coordinator, lost the job she'd had for ten years when the department store for which she worked was purchased by a large retailing conglomerate. The new owners brought in a fashion coordinator (ten years younger than Edythe), and Edythe was so devastated that as she miserably licked her wounds she didn't know what to do next.

"I was paralyzed," she admitted. "I couldn't make a move. Since the field of image consulting was expanding at the time, I eventually thought—in a scattered way— about capitalizing on my fashion background as an independent consultant, and telling women how to package themselves so they would create a good image. I decided to give it a shot, but I really didn't know where to begin."

If you don't know how to start moving:

- Break down decisions into small steps.

Edythe's decision to become an image consultant called for a careful step-by-step implementation. The first thing she needed to do was research the field and find out who her competition was, what products or services they offered, and how they priced themselves.

After the research phase she was ready to get some help in designing and printing business cards and brochures.

The next step was to make some contacts for possible speaking engagements by going through the events sections in newspapers in her area and pulling out names of women's clubs, church groups, and working women's networks. Generally the listings had phone numbers to call for information on meetings, so she'd call and ask for the names of program chairpersons.

Once Edythe had a file of contacts, she devoted an entire month to making cold calls to the contacts to tell them about her work. This approach eventually yielded a few speaking engagements, which in turn led to workshops and a number of individual clients.

Fence Sitters such as Edythe can benefit from a specialized To Do List that pinpoints individual steps, what information is needed to carry forth those steps, and the corresponding deadlines for action. (See Edyth's sample To Do List on page 97.)

4. You're afraid of the unknown.

All too often an unwillingness to deal with change destroys a Fence Sitter's potential for a chance to do better in the future. In the absence of assured results, though, many people tend to put off forever relinquishing the tried for the untried.

Arnie, a Fence-Sitting paralegal, has worked for a two-partner law firm for the past five years. Within the past year, however, a third partner joined the firm, and from the first Arnie and the partner had personality clashes.

"Since he arrived I've spent the whole year thinking of getting out of here," Arnie said, "and when things get tense and I feel stressed I'm convinced it's time for that. But when it comes to acting on it, inertia sets in, since I can't be sure a new firm will be any better than this. In the end I stick with the situation I know as the path of least resistance."

To Arnie, the prospect of giving up the known for the

Fence-Sitter To Do List

Item	Information Needed	Deadline for Action
1. Order Image Consultants Directory	Get address from Connie	Nov. 9
2. Call Eddie re: final artwork approval	Ask Sue when he's getting back from vacation	Nov. 9
3. Get names & #s of program chairs	Order daily paper; save Shoppers	Nov. 15
4. Mail follow-up letters	Check whether I have enough stamps	Nov. 15
5. Think of title for workshop	Talk to Grace for input	Nov. 20
6. Find out if I need insurance	Call agent	Nov. 10
7. Buy larger Rolodex	Borrow stationery store catalogue from Joan	Nov. 25
8. Call in reservation for network meeting	Make sure Kathy can drive	Nov. 11
9. Send Linda flowers when she gets home	Call her at hospital to find out when she's leaving	?
10. Read Color Analysis book		Dec. 1

unknown is a risk he's unwilling to take. But by putting off the decision he's forfeiting the possibility of moving to something new, where his chances and personal relationships might be a great deal better.

If you're afraid of the unknown:

- Pinpoint your fears.

  Since Arnie had already spent so many months trying to make up his mind, my first suggestion was to get right to the heart of the matter by blue-skying what he'd like most in his future, and asking himself what he was most afraid would happen if he left his present job. He quickly earmarked his main priority as freedom from an overdose of daily stress and pinpointed his primary fear—being rejected when he applied for another job. When he acknowledged there would still be alternatives even after one, two, or more rejections (and that the pressure from staying and dealing with the third partner would be worse than the pressure from leaving), I encouraged him to collect the information he needed for job hunting and set a projected date for leaving.

When People Have a Fence-Sitter Style

Sometimes all of us feel shaky about making a decision. And when these times occur even individuals who aren't normally Fence Sitters will adopt this style.

Here are two typical situations.

1. You're not sure that you have enough information.

Many people go through life looking for just one more scrap of information that will help them make up their minds. But since you'll probably never know *everything* about *everything,* it's unlikely you'll ever have all the information you think you must have for each decision. Consequently, waiting till you have it all can be a waste of valuable time.

Jim, a supervising civil engineer who normally would not be characterized as a Fence Sitter, spends hours devising detailed charts whenever he and his wife decide to buy a new household appliance.

"Sometimes I can't believe him!" his wife, Sally, said. "He'll sit at the kitchen table for days comparing makers, models, wholesale costs, retail costs, sales prices, special features, warranty options, and anything else he can think of. Then, after all that, he's still concerned that he doesn't have sufficient information to make the correct choice."

In another case, an elementary-school principal learned a month before a new term was beginning that one of his teachers in the art department had to resign unexpectedly because her husband was being transferred to a permanent overseas job. The principal had to fill the job quickly, so after he interviewed some applicants he was sufficiently decisive to narrow the candidates to two. But then indecision took over.

One applicant was a new college graduate who was filled with enthusiasm and brimming with ideas—and whose manner he liked the most. The other was a fortyish divorcée with two children to support. He felt the latter had a greater need for financial security. And because she had a home in the area and children in the school system, she'd probably be more likely to stay in the job several years. As opposed to this, the young single teacher would have the freedom to pick up and go whenever she saw greener pastures. There was also the factor of teaching experience vs. inexperience. So what was the right decision to make? Which person should he choose?

He decided *not* to make a final decision until he inquired around a bit and gathered more in-depth information on both of the candidates. But in the time he took for that, both candidates found other jobs.

If you think you need more information:

- Be realistic about how much information you really need.

    Granted, time provides chances to study options more fully, and somewhere down the road you could possibly uncover important facts you hadn't considered. But by the same token, as time runs out, options and alternatives can run out, too. Once you know how much information you must have to make a good decision, give yourself a cutoff date.

2. You have too many alternatives to choose from.

When you're faced with a number of alternatives, it's easy to be stuck on the fence. Take Wallace, a superior-court judge who has to make vitally important decisions in the course of his work. He is able to do this so wisely, he receives many accolades. But for something small—like redecorating the kitchen in his bachelor apartment—Wallace, whose hobby is gourmet cooking, became an instant Fence Sitter while trying to choose a laminate for the cabinets and a Formica for the countertop.

"When the contractor spread out what looked like a million chips for me to pick from, my mind went blank," he admitted. "I didn't know how to make a choice because there were so many."

Sometimes even two alternatives are more than people can handle, as Gregg, a director of public relations, discovered when he was approached for two jobs. At the time, Gregg wasn't looking for a job, since he was already running the in-house public-relations department of a large Eastern corporation. But one day a headhunter called with the offer of a spot as public-relations director of a resort hotel in Hawaii—and the very next day Gregg was approached about handling p.r. for his state's department of tourism. The question: Should he keep the job he had or take one of the two others?

If you have too many alternatives to choose from:

• Narrow down your selections as much as possible.

For Wallace that meant choosing the specific laminate chips that would go well with what he already had in his kitchen. I also suggested that when he saw something that would give him the results he wanted, he should immediately stop looking. There might have been something better if he continued to search, but it's certainly not worth his valuable time as a judge to look at every potential combination. This tactic helped Jim as well in choosing his appliances.

Gregg's decision obviously has a greater long-range impact on his life, but the narrowing-down process is essentially the same. Once he determined that he was open to the idea of considering job offers, he had to come up with the criteria by which to compare his choices. The first factor seemed to be geographical location—two of the jobs were in-state, the other almost a continent away. As appealing as Hawaii appeared, Gregg decided not to relocate his family. That left the choice between his current job and the one with the department of tourism. Though the latter seemed to be more interesting because of the new and varied activities involved, it offered a significantly lower rate of pay than Gregg felt he was able to accept. In the end he narrowed down his choice to remaining with his present employer.

Two Important Strategies for Fence Sitters

As we have seen, Fence Sitting can cause much wasted time and energy-draining distress, but there are several strategies that can help.

1. Set firm deadlines.

Decision-making should be broken down into individual steps that continually move you ahead in the process. For example, one Fence-Sitter client, Marvin, who owned a small business, had to decide whether to remain a sole proprietor or take on a business partner. Every time he got close to making the decision, he started to doubt himself and went back to square one to collect more information.

The first thing we did was create a final deadline by which the decision would be made. Next we created "sub-deadlines" for each phase of the decision-making process. You can use a similar process:

Phase 1. Determine objectives   by Jan. 15

Ask yourself what it is you'd like to achieve. Marvin knew that he wanted to expand his business. The question was: Could/should he do it alone?

Phase 2. Get information   by Feb. 1

Collect available facts. Marvin had to determine what degree of capital infusion would be needed to expand and therefore which people might be considered as potential partners.

Phase 3. Clarify alternatives   by Feb. 15

Identify specific courses of action that would meet your objectives. To Marvin, that meant weighing the advantages/disadvantages of going it alone against those of hooking up with the most likely partner prospect.

Phase 4. Make decisions   by Mar. 1

Commit yourself to what seems at the time to be the best course of action. Marvin, after weighing what the loss of his independence would mean against the advantages of additional assistance and support, decided to take on a partner. The partners gave themselves a year in which to evaluate the outcome of their decision, and at that time decided to continue the partnership.

2. Create a ranking system.

This strategy can greatly simplify decision-making. To create one:

1. Set up a chart with several columns categorized according to the things you must take into account when making one or more decisions. The headings for your columns may be different from those in the sample ranking system on page 103, which I

helped a client prepare when she needed to prioritize a list of things to be done. This is because your situation and the decision you have to make may not be based on the same considerations as those in the sample ranking system.

2. When you determine your specific considerations, assign point values to each choice on a scoring scale of 1 to 5 with 1 being "High" and 5 being "Low." In the sample chart the first consideration is the importance of each job, followed by the time required, difficulty, and the possibility of delegating.

3. Compare the points to see what your decision should be.

When I worked with my client Rosalie, who has a high-pressured job as an account executive for a top investment firm, she'd just found out—unexpectedly—that her parents who lived across the country were coming to visit her. Understandably, Rosalie wanted her house to look great for her parents' visit. But there was too much to do and not nearly enough time to do it all in, and Rosalie didn't know where to begin. To allow her to compare her options we used the ranking system strategy, and (1) listed everything she wanted to accomplish; (2) created the separate columns for each factor that would have an impact on what should be done and in what order; and (3) ranked the jobs on the scoring scale of from 1 to 5.

Things to Be Done	Importance of Job to Me	Time required	Difficulty	Could be Delegated	Cost of Delegating
Polish silver	3	1	3	No	——
Cook pâté	1	2	2	No	——
Wash quilt	1	2	2	No	——
Clean refrigerator	3	1	1	Yes	5
Cut grass	1	2	2	Yes	3
Arrange freezer	2	1	2	No	——

When Rosalie finished the chart, we agreed that she would look only at what ranked 1 or 2 in importance to her. Then we scheduled the 1's according to their time and energy requirements, and delegated what she could afford (for instance, cutting the grass). Next we moved on to the 2's. If she ended up with extra time, she could go to the 3's, etc. Even though she knew she wouldn't get to everything, Rosalie felt comfortable and in control as she moved smoothly from one high-priority task to the next.

Additional Strategies and Techniques

1. Check your gut feeling.

Sometimes you have an immediate sense that something is right (or wrong). After checking the pros and cons thoroughly, go back and take a really close look at that gut feeling. If you find that what seems like reasonable choice still makes you uncomfortable, you may want to go with your deeper feelings instead.

2. Pretend you are not the person who has to make the decision.

Imagine that your best friend is asking you for advice on a decision. As you think through the issues with him or her, the fantasy of emotional distance can help you decide more clearly.

3. Talk things over with a friend.

After fantasizing that you are the friend, go back to the real world and approach a good friend if you find you're stuck on a decision. His or her judgment can help make up your own mind.

4. Consider your mood.

Decision-making is difficult when you feel depressed. If possible, hold off making your decisions until your morale improves. You'll find your decisions will be better and much more likely to bring you the end results you desire.

5. Remember that practically every decision will have negatives as well as positives.

Prepare yourself to handle the negatives and then get on with your choice.

6. Toss a coin and go with the results.

When choices seem to be equal, this is the quickest way to proceed. Or as an alternative, write your equal choices on individual slips of paper and toss them into a hat. When you pull one out, accept that choice and give up on the others so you can put your energy and time into the decision you made.

In the final analysis every decision that you make is a chance to gain greater control over your life. You'll accomplish more of what you want to do and waste less energy viewing every option ad infinitum. Naturally, every decision won't work out, but you'll learn something in the process and be able to make a Fence-Sitting style work for you.

Instant Summary for a Fence Sitter

Fence Sitters worry too much about small decisions and can become paralyzed by large ones. Often they don't know what they really want, and even when they do, they're not sure how to go about getting it. These tips can help.

1. Learn to evaluate your needs and desires.
2. Realize that in most situations, there really are no

wrong choices. Any outcome, good or bad, will give you feedback that you can use to improve your decision-making abilities.

3. Break down your decisions into a series of small steps with individual deadlines.
4. Pinpoint your fears so that you can deal with them directly.
5. Use a ranking system when comparing a number of different alternatives.
6. Get input from a knowledgeable friend.
7. Pay attention to your instincts—your gut feeling.
8. Take time to relax and reward yourself along the way.

CHAPTER 8

Cliff Hanger

*I usually wait until the last minute
to start work.*

Sandy, a Cliff-Hanger artist and parent of three boys, has gone through life rebelling against her mother's reminders—as well as her nagging deadlines—to keep her room in order. "If it wasn't 'Before your father comes home' it was always 'Before you go out to play' or 'Before company comes,'" she said as she looked at her present-day cluttered kitchen with the easel and paints at one end. "So I always said that when I grew up and got a place of my own, I was going to keep it *my* way just to show her a thing or two.

"As long as I have my children and art, I don't care about the house," she said. "I deliberately put off straightening up until I have company coming. Then I shove things into the closets five minutes before they arrive.

"My mother thinks this is terrible, but I don't really care."

As Sandy's reaction indicates, Cliff Hanging—postponing action on something we have decided or need to do—can have complex emotional roots. There are many times when people do it. Some, like Sandy, wait to start a task when they feel hostile, angry, or resentful toward an authority figure in the past. Others consciously or unconsciously like to set themselves up with eleventh-hour obstacles. They like racing through the final-hour rush trying to beat the clock. Still others put off the initial step when there's no gratification for them until they complete the entire job. And many simply resist structured living—and dates and times when things should be done.

Are You a Cliff Hanger?

To find out if Cliff Hanging is one of your organizational styles, take the following quiz. As you answer Never (N), Occasionally (O), or Frequently (F), rate yourself according to the following scale.

Never	*Occasionally*	*Frequently*
0 points	1 point	2 points

N O F

1. I delay until the eleventh hour before beginning important projects.
2. I need to have outside time pressure to complete a task.
3. I find myself dashing out of the door most mornings to catch my ride.
4. I feel that stress helps me to be more alert and to think clearly and perceptively.
5. I tend to get bored when things are going too smoothly.
6. I run around in a last-minute rush at least a couple of times a week.
7. I wait until the last call to buy gifts.
8. I involve others in a race to help me meet deadlines.
9. I feel exhilarated after completing an important business deal or project just before the deadline.
10. I have more motivation and drive when I have outside pressure.

Totals:

0–6 points	You're not really a Cliff Hanger.
7–13 points	You have strong Cliff Hanging tendencies.
14–20 points	You're a full-fledged Cliff Hanger.

Why You're a Cliff Hanger

In working with many Cliff Hangers I have found, in addition to the emotional roots, the following reasons behind this organizational style.

1. They estimate their time inaccurately.

Cliff Hangers have difficulty understanding the inflexible nature of time. They can visualize the final result of a project, but they fail to think about how long it will take to achieve that result. Therefore they seldom plan for things going wrong or being more difficult than anticipated.

Alexandra, a Cliff-Hanger magazine writer, constantly relies upon winging it rather than planning her work. Because she's unrealistic she invariably says, "This will take two weeks," when in the past similar assignments have taken over a month.

For a while she thrived on her last-minute push and deadline-to-deadline living. But on the day I visited her, the sense of urgency that motivated her to work was rapidly turning to strain. With too many deadlines confronting her and too little time to meet them, she was finally acknowledging that her stress was causing her to be counterproductive.

Sometimes she was making her deadlines with a breath to spare. But more and more she was missing them as at the final moment things piled up like cars in a freeway crash. Murphy's Law had come into play, and

Alexandra was facing the truth that when she reached her deadline time she never ended up with the time she had anticipated.

"I had a terrific assignment for a medical article," she said, "but the whole thing hinged on interviews with three epidemiologists. My editor wanted a story based on their latest research, so she gave me a one-month deadline to get the story in.

"After three weeks, however, she called and said she needed the material now because she'd learned a rival publication was scheduling a similar story. She offered to work with me on the piece so we could get it done. But since I hadn't started it, there was nothing with which to work. I frantically phoned the three scientists to get some quick interviews, but all of them were out of town and I couldn't reach even one. The entire project went down the drain—and I lost a friendly editor and lucrative magazine."

If you estimate your time inaccurately:

• Pay attention to the reality of time flow.

When Alexandra conceded that inattention to time was causing many of her problems, our first step was to help her become aware of the passage of time. I asked her to estimate how long each of the new assignments on her desk should take, based on the length of time others like them had taken. I then advised her (1) to break down the assignment into all its steps to get a clearer picture of everything involved; (2) to actually time herself when she started working; and (3) to keep an accurate on-paper record of that time so that in the future she could compare her estimates with reality. This would enable her to project more closely the hours her future work would demand.

Together we worked on the Cliff Hanger's specialized To Do List (see page 112) and set up two deadlines—a "Should Be Done By" and an "Absolute Deadline." If you have Alexandra's problem, this will work for you too because it encourages you to focus on the "Should Be Done By" deadline as the ideal date by which you would like to complete something. At the same time this deadline gives you room to spare as a safety precaution. Should you miss "Should Be Done By" for any reason, such as interruptions, disruptions, limitations on your energy, and other similar factors, you still have the "Absolute Deadline"—at which time you know you must complete something. (Note: Many Cliff Hangers will be tempted to ignore "Should Be Done By." But its purpose is to alert them to the reality of time flow and warn them that "Absolute Deadline" leaves no room for contingencies. This is a concept of planning that Cliff Hangers often miss.)

2. They thrive on stress.

Some Cliff Hangers look forward to adrenaline surges—and the push this gives them to meet a commitment just in the nick of time. They enjoy living in the pressure-cooker climate that accompanies a last-minute frenzy, and they like the high produced by the adrenaline that their body releases.

When Cliff Hangers are able to control this adrenaline-sparked stress, they often can come through and avoid confronting disaster. When stress is overwhelming, however, and fraught with anxiety, it can cause real problems.

"That's the state that I'm in now," said Blake, a campaign manager for a gubernatorial candidate. "I was delighted when I got this job. I love the excitement of lots to do and just making it in time, and I was also pleased at the thought of travel and constant interaction with people. But now I'm so frenzied, I'm out of my mind trying to do everything.

"Just as a few examples, I make all of the candidate's travel plans, set up his speaking engagements, arrange meetings with local and county leaders, and serve as liaison to the press. I need tons of information both for and from my candidate. Yet nobody gets me anything so I

Sample Cliff-Hanger To Do List

Item	Should Be Done By	Absolute Deadline
1. Set up file for research for projected article on sleep	End of month	Open
2. Write Lynn about statistics on sleep disorders	Oct. 14	Oct. 22
3. Call Judy with additions she wants from dream article	Today	Today
4. Continue with current assignment on problem employees and try to draft four pages	Nov. 16 for whole article	Nov. 30
5. Follow up on request for interview with Dr. Barrows	Oct. 21	Oct. 28
6. Read proofs for article on friendship and call John's assistant with any corrections	Today	End of week
7. Make lunch date with new editor at XXX magazine	Today	End of week
8. Type up draft of ideas for him	Oct. 5	Oct. 7
9. Check in library to see what else has been done on those ideas. Revise draft if necessary. Retype.	Oct. 7	Oct. 9
10. Listen to tape of interview with Dr. Congers and transcribe quotes and info I need for problem employees assignment.	Oct. 21	Oct. 31

have it when I need it, and everyone pushes me constantly to do last-minute things.

"I'm normally able to function well in this kind of environment. But with this job too many things involve last-minute hassles. The stress is so upsetting it's beginning to get me down."

If you thrive on stress, but find it works against you at times:

- Move up deadlines.
  As Blake and I talked—and he told me more about his problems of getting information he needed when he needed it—I showed him how to move up deadlines on his calendar so he'd stand a greater chance of obtaining the material on time. By setting up firm early deadlines for what he required to do his job, he'd be better equipped to arrange the travel plans, speaking engagements, meetings, and press conferences without waiting till the eleventh hour. Through doing this Blake was eventually able to handle his job so the stress was no longer threatening.

3. They think they need pressure in order to perform.

The "I work best under pressure" belief causes many Cliff Hangers to put things off because they're convinced they need to feel pressure—from themselves or from someone else—in order to do anything.

For years Alan worked at a nine-to-five job in an accounting firm before he decided to go on his own. Through previous weekend moonlighting he felt that he had some contacts, so he set up an office in his home, convinced he'd devised the perfect way to pursue his career. But after three months he called me and said he'd found that to get down to work, he needed the pressure of a boss constantly monitoring him.

"At home I wait to get psyched up before getting started," he said, "and while I've been waiting, the tax forms have piled up. Now that the deadline is right around the corner, I have to almost skim over the work and I don't have time to review it for adjustments that would improve it. I feel on the brink of disaster—and I've only just begun."

Fortunately, Alan saw immediately that if he wanted to work on his own and have a successful business, he needed to eliminate putting off tasks while he waited to get inspired. I encouraged him to force himself to start a task even if he wasn't in the ideal mood.

If you think you need pressure in order to perform:

- Use the Five-Minute Plan.

    In this plan you commit yourself to begin work on a task for only five minutes. At the end of this period you decide whether you want to continue for the next five minutes. Once you initiate action, you tend to keep going until you get tired, are interrupted, or the task is completed.

    The Five-Minute Plan is especially helpful when you find yourself avoiding something unpleasant as well. Often the anticipation of an unpleasant task is worse than the task itself. You end up spending more energy worrying about it than you would just doing it. But even though you know that you'll feel better when the unpleasant task is no longer hanging over your head, it still can be difficult to get started. Knowing that you're committing yourself for just five minutes gives you an easy out if you need it. This simple psychological trick worked for Alan. It enabled him to get over that first threatening hurdle and ease into his work gradually without waiting for pressure to force him into action.

How You Can Make a Tendency Toward Cliff Hanging Work for You

Not all procrastination must be overcome, since some delays are appropriate in the context of their situation. But regardless of your reason for delays, make sure that you allow yourself enough time to do a decent job by following these four strategies:

1. Break down a job assignment and figure out the steps required to reach the end point of the job. Then estimate the time each individual step will take.

Once you decide what the end point of your work should be, what's required to get there, and the time each individual step will take, count down from the deadline date of a job to determine how many days or hours the total job—and each step—will require. In this way you can determine the last possible starting date that will get you to your deadline on time.

Ray is the assistant to the director of a telephone company's free-lecture bureau. He's responsible for drafting the speeches, as well as the film presentations company representatives give to organizations. He's also a perfect example of someone who appropriately delays starting a job until the eleventh hour.

When Ray was hired, he soon observed that the longer the director had to produce a speech, the more changes he liked to make. And often after these back-and-forth changes, the final version the director approved was amazingly close to the first draft Ray submitted.

Because of this Ray holds back on turning in a draft till close to deadline to avoid unnecessary work. Then when he knows he should get to work he uses end-point scheduling to successfully figure out through an accurate on-paper record what he must do to draft an effective speech, and how many days he'll need to do it. This end-point scheduling procedure can work well for all Cliff Hangers. Here is Ray's projected schedule.

		Starting Date
1. Research and obtain material	3 days	March 1-3
2. Lay out speech or film commentary	1 day	March 4
3. Do first rough draft	3 days	March 5-7
4. Revise draft and recheck facts	2 days	March 8-9
5. Polish and have typed	1 day	March 10

2. Monitor your time as you work.

By doing this you will be able to redesign time frames if necessary whenever you add new items to your To Do List. Simultaneously, monitoring will provide gratification as you count up the number of concrete hours you're actually working toward your goal. It will also help you to see that you're making insufficient progress if, say, you're only spending an hour a week on a goal that will take forty hours.

3. Recognize the attainment of mini-goals as you go along.

By rewarding yourself with some small pleasure each time you complete a mini-goal, you'll encourage yourself to keep moving forward.

4. Periodically revise your Master To Do List to make sure that you aren't putting off the really critical items.

If you stay in touch with your priorities, you can procrastinate "safely" by only delaying on the less significant tasks.

Because of its deep emotional roots, Cliff Hanging can be difficult to work with at times. But every success that you achieve in restructuring negative Cliff Hanging habits will reduce the stress and problems in your life and enable you to live with this style in a positive and productive way.

Instant Summary for a Cliff Hanger

When you repeatedly wait until the last minute to start major tasks and projects, you run an ever increasing risk that you'll turn in substandard work or even miss your deadline completely. However, if you enjoy the surge of adrenaline that comes with Cliff Hanging, you can learn to avert the inevitable disaster by doing the following:

1. Become aware of how long things really take and monitor your time as you work.
2. Don't wait for inspiration in order to begin a task. Schedule a time to start or try the Five-Minute Plan.
3. Create mini-goals to help you feel satisfied about your progress.
4. Move up deadlines.
5. Check your Master To Do List to make sure that you aren't putting off the critical items. If you feel like procrastinating, do it with only the smaller, less significant jobs.
6. Take time to relax and reward yourself along the way.

CHAPTER 9

Put Your Space in Order

How can I keep from losing things?

Just as it was necessary to refresh yourself on the basic principles of time management before reading the Time-style chapter, it's equally essential to review space-management basics-for-everyone before going into the Space-style chapters. In this way you can see how the general principles of space organization—the environment in which you live and work—can be custom-designed to match your personal style or styles.

In the first half of this chapter we'll deal with space management in both your home and job. In the second we'll focus exclusively on organizing space in your workplace.

Why We Have Space Problems

On my initial visits to clients they almost invariably greet me with "I bet this is the worst mess you ever saw!" But when you're involved in a great many things it's almost humanly impossible to have a mess-free existence. Most of us experience this problem because either we collect too many possessions we don't need, or we fail to use our existing space in the most effective way.

A so-called "mess" in itself needn't be a problem, however, if everything in it has a specific place and can be put there quickly and easily. But when your things have no specific place (and aren't put away in that place) chaotic houses and workplaces can be very distracting.

The same thing is true of unneeded items you've kept around for years because you have never determined that it's time to get rid of them. A choreographer who consulted me lives in a one-room apartment where all kinds of assorted objects are stuck anywhere—and everywhere—"just temporarily." And a draftsman who has vacationed in every state in the union has keepsakes from all fifty of them gathering dust in his office.

As our lives change, most of us find our needs and wants change, too, until we inevitably reach the point when we have neither the physical (nor mental) space to accommodate our proliferated belongings. When that time comes, you'll benefit from organizing your space because:

1. You'll save time by not having to waste it trying to locate things.
2. You'll save money since time spent looking for lost items can change from minutes to dollars when you hold up an important meeting at work (or a community-service meeting in your home) to look for a misplaced clipping or address.
3. You'll be more productive, effective, and creative because, even though some creative people believe order and creativity don't mix, the confidence that comes with knowing where things are when you need them stimulates creativity.

Evaluating and Assessing What You Own

Your first step is a hard look at your possessions to decide what value they have to you today. Use the following where to start/assessment exercise.

Take a walk around your home or office and note:

1. What you currently have.
2. How it is organized and stored.

3. How you maintain those organizational systems.

Next, ask yourself:

1. Do I like what I have?
2. Is each item conveniently placed or stored?
3. Is it easy to put things away?

Clearing Out

Depending on the way you like to work, you can clear out one area at a time—or attack your entire home or office with a full-scale clearing out. It may seem overwhelming at first. But this is a normal reaction. To get started:

1. Work when you're in the mood. It's easier to make decisions about what and what not to keep.
2. Block out segments of time according to your tolerance level (e.g., one half hour, one half day, successive weekends).
3. Move from the first room to the second (if you're doing a full-scale clearing out) only after the first has been completely sorted through. Within each room, move in a clockwise direction so that no area is skipped.
4. Use a large wastebasket. This encourages you to keep going. A small one may fill up too quickly.
5. Ask yourself of every item you own:
   • Does it have a current or specifically planned future usefulness?
   • Does it have value to me—sentimental, monetary, aesthetic?
   • Would it be difficult or expensive to replace?
   • Is it taking up space that could serve a better purpose in my life today?

It's often *hard* to get rid of things you've had around for a while, even if they have no great value. But here are pointers that will help you get through this successfully.

1. First, separate what you would like to save from what you are prepared to part with. If you have real trouble unloading yesteryear's "treasures," take a picture of them. In this way you'll have their memories—and they won't take up storage space.
2. Next, divide the items you're getting rid of into the following categories:
   • Garbage
   • Relatives/friends
   • Charity
   • For Sale (to be sold at a planned garage sale, flea market, etc.)

After your home-and-office clearing out, clearing out your clothing will be a separate activity, and for this you need to ask yourself a different set of questions.

As you answer the questions remember that (1) clothing deteriorates with age, (2) items become dated, and (3) the odds are great that many things you save will never look as good or stylish as when you first began pushing them to the side of the rack. Keep only those clothes that meet the following criteria:

1. Do they make you feel and look good?
2. Do they reflect your personality and the image you'd like to project?
3. Are they in good condition/repair?
4. Do they fit well?

After Your Full-Scale Clearing Out

Once you start putting your space in order by paring down your possessions, you can keep it under control by asking yourself these questions before you buy or take on new items:

1. Will I really use this?
2. Do I want it badly enough to care for it?
3. Am I prepared to get rid of something I already own in order to make room for it?
4. Where exactly will I put it?

What Makes a Good Storage System?

Managing space efficiently does not necessarily mean making it neat. Rather, it means making it functional by—as already pointed out—assigning everything you own a practical place, and getting into the habit of returning things where they belong.

To make it as easy as possible to do this, you need to design a storage arrangement so that you—and the people around you, if need be—can understand and use your system. Starting with your existing storage space and working within its boundaries:

1. Group similar items together so it's easy to see if something is missing or if you have a duplication.
2. Put the things that you use most often close to you and those you use less often farther away.
3. Place those that you use frequently on top of or in front of your categorized groups, or hang them on a wall so they're easy to reach.

If you still need more room after you make the best use of your existing space, a wide array of ready-made space extenders is available in stores and catalogues. But before you invest time and money:

1. Determine what you really need. For example, do you need additional/improved storage for files? For books? For work in progress? For clothes? For kitchen equipment? For tools? For whatever?
2. Measure the space where you plan to put a space extender. (For example, is your desktop large

enough to accommodate a large vertical rack with ten partitions?)
3. Make sure whatever you buy is appropriate for your organizational style.

You don't need fancy, expensive equipment to do the job. In fact, too many people make the mistake of buying all sorts of commercial organizing products in the mistaken belief that these products in and of themselves will automatically organize them. Unfortunately, this won't happen—if you don't think before you buy.

What Your Space Arrangements Say About You

In addition to being functional, the environment in which you live and work is a reflection of you and your personal style—and especially in the workplace the image your space projects will influence how you're perceived by your boss, coworkers, and clients.

1. Your furniture arrangement conveys your accessibility and the degree of formality or informality you expect. (Sitting in a conversation area with your visitors, for instance, will usually put them more at ease than facing them from behind your desk.)
2. The top of your desk and decorative items and mementos around the room—such as pictures, books, hobby equipment, appropriate cartoons, and awards—tell a great deal about what's important to you.
3. The more tidy your office, the more others will feel you have things under control.

How to Organize Your
Workplace for Your
Personal Style and Efficiency

Ideally you should always have:

- Good lighting that falls where you need it
- Furniture that's functional and scaled to the size of the room
- Equipment that *works*
- Chairs that are the right height
- A certain amount of privacy if possible
- Music or white noise to shut out irritating background sounds

In addition, here are four other tips:

1. Set things up with an eye toward convenience.

Convenience is a top priority, as Ben, the head medical-records technician at a citywide health center, learned.

As long as he had a sufficiently large desk to hold all of his papers, Ben paid little attention to office arrangements. Because of this, when he had to switch offices, he quickly moved in his furniture without concerning himself about where it was placed. As a result, he put his desk across the room from the wall-mounted pencil sharpener that was already there.

The many pencils Ben used, however, needed frequent sharpening, and he found himself periodically trooping across the room. This inconvenience soon played havoc with Ben's working schedule. The simple, obvious solution was relocating the pencil sharpener next to Ben's desk.

2. Subdivide your space to create a specific location for each task you do.

It's helpful to divide your office into separate sections that correspond with your work—a place for routine paperwork, a place for heavy concentration, a place for chatting, a place for storage.

Sherri is a medical illustrator—and also the art director—for a health publication. As director, Sherri must administer a department, do extensive paperwork, and interview free-lance artists seeking work. She needs sufficient space to handle these tasks—and since she does many illustrations herself, she needs "private" space to think and create.

"When I took this job, the disorganization in this office made it hard to concentrate," she said. "It seemed as though I wasted part of each day just clearing things away so the artists who came in had a place to sit and display their portfolios. I wasted my creative energy, too, by always having to look for supplies before I sat down at the drawing board to do my own illustrations."

Ultimately Sherri made her small office more workable by dividing it into separate sections that complemented each job she did. In one corner she arranged her desk and a table at right angles for desktop space and desk-drawer storage as well as a place to interview artists.

In the opposite corner from her desk, Sherri set up her drawing board and enclosed it with bookcases to store art supplies. This semi-private area allowed her to be quietly creative without disrupting the other work in progress on her desk.

3. Make good use of color.

Your color scheme should reflect your personality and taste and be a background you're comfortable living with. Ross is a literary agent who runs his business from his city apartment, and everything about his office/living room is an extension of him. He uses color to make himself feel good and project a certain image. Since he likes to think of himself as cool and sophisticated, he chose a blue and green color scheme for the entire apartment.

A pale blue velvet sofa with a high, curved back separates the living room from the office space, and everything in the office is done in varying shades of blue with touches of green for highlights. His desk is an oblong glass table, and as a contrast to the glass-top desk, Ross uses a cut-down oak dining table for a combination coffee-

and-conference table and for spreading out manuscripts. It's a room Ross is pleased to show off.

To use color for your style and image keep the following things in mind:

- Red, yellow, and orange suggest warmth.
- Blue and green offer coolness.
- White is sterile (though it increases the impact of light).
- Beige and earth tones are neutral, but can be boring.
- An overdose of black is usually too drastic, unless it's done for dramatic effect.

4. Be sure your office looks professional.

The home office of a free-lance writer need not be as formal as the corporate office of a finance director. But all work space should reflect the professionalism of the people working there.

Chris had been a vocational counselor in her first years of work. But while she was home caring for her children, she decided that when she went back to work she'd go into marriage counseling. Later, after returning to school and becoming certified, she found a spot as a marriage counselor in a family counseling service.

Her office was a cubbyhole (and forlorn and cold to boot) so Chris proceeded to make it warm by decorating the walls with snapshots of her children, drawings and crafts they made in school, and greeting cards they'd sent her for birthdays, and holidays.

On her desk was a loudly painted pencil holder her daughter had made in Girl Scouts, and papers and books were strewn all over because she generally didn't allow enough time to put her things away. There were also plastic containers from her lunches since she seldom remembered to toss them out.

Basically Chris's space problem stemmed from the fact that she was so involved in her work that once she set up her work space, she never really *saw* it again until the counseling service was scheduled to have an open house for its board of directors. At that point a caring colleague mentioned the need for "professional offices to impress the board of directors" and suggested that maybe—to be prepared—Chris take a second look at hers.

She took awhile to get things in order. But with the help of her colleague Chris was able to streamline her work space, and get rid of what made the office look like a family room at home. There was little she could do with the cold metal desk her employers refused to change. But she warmed it up with fresh flowers and straw baskets for the books and papers. To replace the worn green plastic chairs that were formerly in the office, she next had the counseling service purchase two chairs with colorful cushions for clients.

Now with plants on the shelves and files and materials arranged conveniently within them, Chris is productive, effective, and creative—and proud of a warm and inviting workplace that reflects *her* personal style in a professional way.

Space-Style Quiz

The following quiz will help you identify your style(s) of managing space. It's okay to have more than one answer per question because many people are a combination of styles. For example, if your answers are mostly As, you're primarily an Everything Out. If your answers are mostly Cs, you're primarily a Right Angler. If you have an equal combination of both, you're a mix of those two styles. The key at the end of the quiz will direct you to the chapters that discuss your primary styles.

1. When I go through my in box at work, I:
   a. Tack everything onto my bulletin board that needs to be done.
   b. Quickly sort and stash everything out of view.

    c. Subdivide the contents into neatly arranged piles.

    d. Save everything, including junk mail, which might come in handy as scrap paper.

    e. Just dump the contents wherever I can find room.

2. When I have an important telephone call to make, I:

    a. Write a reminder to myself and keep it in plain view.

    b. Enter the information I need in a notebook.

    c. Make sure that wherever I put the reminder it looks straight and pleasing to view.

    d. Add the task to my many To Do lists.

    e. Jot a note on the corner of a magazine, a napkin, the palm of my hand, or whatever is nearby.

3. When I receive catalogs and mailings, I:

    a. Leave them out so I will not forget to order.

    b. Put them away in a drawer so I will not be distracted by them.

    c. Place them next to similarly sized catalogs on the shelf or perfectly centered on a desk or table.

    d. Add them to the heap of catalogs from the past six years.

    e. Toss them in the first spot that comes to mind.

4. When I get my monthly bills, I:

    a. Leave them in an obvious place so I will not forget to pay them.

    b. Put them into folders and file them in a cabinet.

    c. Keep them in neat little piles with squared-off edges.

    d. Mix them in with sales receipts, credit slips, refund forms, and any other financial information I may need someday.

    e. Scatter them throughout the house till they're nearly impossible to find.

Key: a. Everything Out b. Nothing Out c. Right Angler d. Pack Rat e. Total Slob

CHAPTER 10

Everything Out

*I prefer to have everything out where
I can see it all.*

Hugh Kenner, professor of English at Johns Hopkins University, wrote in *Discover* magazine: "Consider my desk. I take a reference book from a shelf. Knowing I will refer to it again soon, I leave it on my desk for now. And this letter inviting me to a conference. I'll leave it next to the book for now because I'll be referring to it when I make travel arrangements. These notes for the essay I'm writing—I turn to them frequently, so I'll leave them here for now."

"I'll put it here for now, so I can see it" is the motto for Everything Outs—people who think that out of sight is out of mind and who believe they work best when everything they need is right out in the open.

When I visited Rob, a staff photographer for a sports magazine, he had an office/workroom where his desk and tables were covered with negatives, black-and-white prints, color transparencies, contact sheets, cover shots, in-progress photo features, and cameras and projectors. The walls of the room were basic—their only covering was a single coat of flat paint—except for the wall near the telephone which was full of the scribbled numbers for photo labs, model agencies, and people he frequently called. He and his staff thought it was great to keep the numbers in a place where they couldn't possibly lose them.

"We call it our 'functional graffiti,'" Rob laughed.

Since Rob liked his graffiti so much and didn't plan

129

to recover the walls, there was no need to change his
system. But unfortunately, for many Everything Outs,
keeping things out in plain view does *not* mean that they
can always find what they're looking for. More often
they discover that as layer covers layer, the clutter gets
to be too much and they can't remember where they put
things "for now."

Are You an Everything Out?

To find out if Everything Out is one of your organizational styles, take the following quiz. As you answer
Never (N), Occasionally (O), or Frequently (F), rate
yourself according to the following scale.

Never	Occasionally	Frequently
0 points	1 point	2 points

                                                        N   O   F

1. Do you prefer having things out where
   you can see them?
2. Do you jot down notes on whatever
   piece of paper catches your eye?
3. Do you feel as though it's a waste of
   time to put things away in drawers and
   closets if you're going to use them
   again?
4. Do you believe that out of sight is out
   of mind?
5. Do you like to surround yourself with
   pictures, inspirational thoughts, children's drawings, cartoons, etc.?
6. When you're working on a project, do
   you prefer to spread out everything
   you might need and leave it all there
   until you're finished?

7. Do you forget about things that you put away?
8. Do you see piles as evidence you're working hard?
9. When filing papers, do you worry that you may never see them again?
10. Do you like things to stare you in the face so you'll be reminded of what you have to do?

_____

Totals:

0–6 points	You're not really an Everything Out.
7–13 points	You have strong Everything-Out tendencies.
14–20 points	You're a full-fledged Everything Out.

Paper Processing—If You're an Everything Out

If you score from 7 to 20 points in the foregoing quiz, paper processing is undoubtedly one of your major problems. When this is the case—and you don't know what to do with incoming papers—they soon start piling up till the stacks grow so high you worry that there's something in there that you've forgotten about that is going to "get" you. It's true that some productive people deliberately stack their papers on their desks, and know what and where everything is. But most people operate better without mile-high piles that make finding things an exercise in frustration.

Generally when clients call me in to help organize their paperwork, they explain their accumulations with:

• "I had no place to put this, so it's here temporarily."
• "I'm afraid I'll forget to do this if I don't leave it out."
• "I may need this in the future so I've stuck it here."

Behind these paperwork-crisis statements is a problem of decision-making. My clients are really saying:

- "I can't handle this right now. What should I do with it?"
- "I don't have the answer to this. What should I do with it?"
- "I just finished with this. What should I do with it?"

Every paper that lands on your desk has to go somewhere or be acted upon in some way, so you need to form the habit of sorting whatever comes in. The advantage of sorting is that the next time you have to find something, you (usually) won't have to go through every piece of paper. You'll only have to go through the pile in the category where it would have been placed.

The following is a simple, basic sorting system. Begin by labeling seven containers or designated areas:

INCOMING	TO FILE
OUTGOING	TO READ
TRASH	TO DO
	PENDING

Select a basket or tray, or designate one corner of your desk, as your INCOMING spot. Unless you specifically authorize it, nothing coming into your office goes anywhere else. Sit at your desk with your Incoming pile in front of you. As you work your way down the pile, ask yourself of each individual paper, "What is this?" Then follow the diagram on page 134. Remember: Once you take a paper out of your Incoming box, never put it back. Forward it at least one step by putting it in the appropriate category.

One final suggestion: To make sure your To Do container does not turn into a permanent residence for some of your paperwork, go through it on a regular basis and prioritize what needs to be done. When you do this, either (1) arrange the papers themselves as your reminder of what needs to be done; or (2) decide what action the paper requires you to take and enter that on your prioritized To Do list. Then place the original paper back in the box or in a separate To Do folder of papers that are awaiting action as you move forward on your To Do list.

Devoting a few minutes a day to handling your To Do's generally works much better than waiting to get to it in an elusive two hours every two weeks or so. However, if under some circumstances you get behind on your To Do's, try to set aside a day or half a day to get them back in shape. Also, don't forget to schedule time for following up items that are pending, as well as those you've referred or delegated to others. Use your calendar for this.

Unfortunately, as soon as you finish processing one batch of paperwork, more comes in with the tide. But the following three tips can help to reduce this inevitable paperwork flow:

1. Have your mail screened to eliminate the junk.
2. Don't ask for unnecessary or lengthy reports.
3. Transmit messages and information verbally whenever you can.

In addition, take yourself off of mailing lists. The less paper that comes to you, the less time you'll have to spend dealing with it.

Why and When People Are Everything Outs

Certain situations encourage people to be Everything Outs. Some persons make these situations positives. Others turn them into negatives. Note whether you see yourself in any of these situations.

1. They like seeing jobs that have to be done staring them in the face.

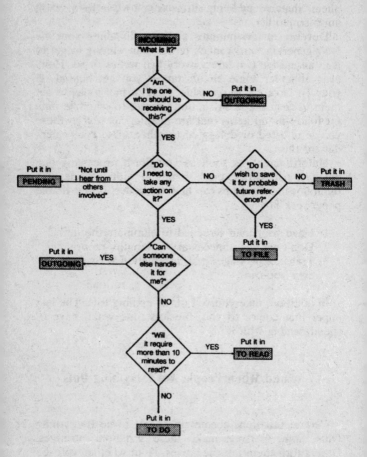

INCOMING
"What is it?"

"Am I the one who should be receiving this?" — NO → Put it in OUTGOING

↓ YES

Put it in PENDING ← "Not until I hear from others involved" — "Do I need to take any action on it?" — NO → "Do I wish to save it for probable future reference?" — NO → Put it in TRASH

↓ YES (future reference) Put it in TO FILE

↓ YES (action)

Put it in OUTGOING ← YES — "Can someone else handle it for me?"

↓ NO

"Will it require more than 10 minutes to read?" — YES → Put it in TO READ

↓ NO

Put it in TO DO

Maria, a fiber artist, kept all her current canvases and supplies stacked against one wall, and all of the paperwork for job commissions on a bulletin board above them. She enjoyed being surrounded by this and working in this muddle until—when she called me in for help—all of her materials were on top of one another and leaning precariously against the walls. When I asked her to write down a few of the goals she eventually hoped to attain as a result of our working together, the first goal she wrote was "Things will not fall when moved."

2. They're living through a time of pressure (or rush).

Guy, a pharmacist who lives alone in an apartment he has set up on his own, is experiencing a great deal of stress following his recent divorce. Because he pays alimony and child support, he is short on money. Instead of buying new things, he has to salvage what he can from the home he'd shared with his wife. Most of the items need repairs, so he keeps an entire table near the front door crowded with things that need fixing that he doesn't want to forget. Among the items are a cord from a toaster, a dictating machine without batteries, an heirloom candelabra that has a broken base, one shoe that needs a heel, and a wall clock that doesn't run.

3. They have no real space to put things away.

Beth lives in a tiny apartment and therefore has to be an Everything Out. She teaches voice, and to keep track of her students, as well as her own singing job possibilities, she covered one entire wall with cork and uses this wall for pinning up sheet music, publicity photos, notes, addresses, greeting cards, sales slips, cleaners' stubs, other people's business cards, and pages from trade publications.

On the other walls she hangs hats, tote bags, purses, pots and pans, and an innovative three-column To Do List with a separate heading for three columns. The first column is marked TO DO, the second DOING, and the third, DONE. Individual index cards for everything she has to do are tacked under the To Do column, and later while she's doing (or as she completes a job) the index cards are moved around. For example, prior to having new publicity pictures taken, she had "Get new publicity pictures" on an index card under To Do. When the appointment was set up, the card was moved to Doing. Then when the pictures were in, she moved the card to Done. It's a busy-looking system but it works—so Beth is a positive Everything Out.

Strategies and Products for Everything Outs

If you find that you identify with Rob, Maria, Guy, or Beth, there are strategies and products that will help you.

1. A prime strategy is organizing your desk area by doing a desktop survey every six months (or when you haven't seen the surface for a while).

As you look at every item on your desk, ask:

1. Do I like it?
2. Is it functional?
3. Is this the best place for it?

If your answer is no, either move it to a better spot, fix it, give it away, or toss it.

When you're ready to select products, the accessories you choose will naturally depend on the work that you do and how many of the items on the market you have space for and need. But the right accessories will play a big part in getting you organized, so consider obtaining some of the following. All have been selected with the idea of maximum visibility in mind. Most come in assorted colors you can match to your decor.

- **Open Plastic Desk Trays** that can be used either singly or stacked to any height to organize current papers.
- **Pencil Container** for your favorite pens and pencils (not those that are broken or out of ink!).
- **Stationery Caddy.** Generally this item has about four different-sized compartments and can conveniently hold pads of paper, address books, postcards, etc.
- **Alphabetized Telephone/Address File** with a hinged see-through dustcover. Get a size that will accommodate business cards so you don't have to spend time copying over the information.
- **Workstation Organizer.** This is a unit of organized storage space which increases available work space because these units leave your desk clear while keeping your materials organized and accessible at the rear of your desk.
- **Vertical Rack** for separating categories of papers in active projects. These racks come in heavy-duty metal or inexpensive plastic sections that can be added to if you want to enlarge the system.
- **Post-It Notes and Tray.** These handy pads are available in different sizes—either plain or with a humorous message—and because they stick to almost any surface, they eliminate the need for paper clips. Note trays that take minimal space on your desk are useful for sorting and storing them.
- **Mounted Coil Pens.** These pens with adhesive backing and stretch cords can be attached to your phone or anywhere else where you have difficulty keeping a pen.

Once your desk is set up—if you *still* have an overflow—you can buy small or large stackable bins (available in housewares departments) and place them near your desk. A three-basket storage cart is another way to keep current projects at hand, and upright roll files placed near your desk provide appropriately sized storage space for plans and drawings.

2. Use your wall space effectively.

- Put up a bulletin board or tack up corkboard or burlap to convert your wall into an information or message center.

  Be sure, however, to decide whether the display areas you set up on them will be used for (1) reminders of upcoming dates and events, or (2) general interests, such as pictures of friends, quotes, posters, and memorabilia. Never mix the two or your reminders will fade into a distracting collage. If you must use the same display area, use a broad piece of tape to divide the area in two.

- Buy individual Lucite wall pockets (molded plastic containers, letter or legal size) that attach either to the wall with screws or magnetically to a metal surface.

  They will organize your papers and projects in a visible, easy-to-reach system that keeps your desk clear for working.

- Use slanted tier racks (multiple wall pockets joined together) for arranging magazines and different kinds of display literature.

- Install vinyl-coated steel shelves for additional wall storage space.

- Hang calendars that provide the amount of space you need for advance planning—month by month or the entire year at a glance.

- Hang chalkboards or drawing boards (which can be used with colored markers or magnetic pieces) to post updates on project performance or for informal notes and reminders.

3. Use color coding.

Brilliant color coding that permits quick identification is especially good for Everything Outs because the colors provide such quick visual cues. This system serves two purposes.

First, you don't have to stop and read a written heading to determine category grouping. As a result, it will take you far less time to go through a subset of twenty green folders than it will to sort through fifty plain manila folders spread out on the floor. It's also a great guarantee against misfiling.

Second, as you sort and classify paperwork (or the various activities and interests in your life), different colors for different types help you keep track of things and maintain a balance between them. For example, for your activities and interests you might color-code your appointment book/calendar as follows:

> Green   activities related to your work
> Red   spare-time, social, and leisure activities
> Blue   personal/family activities

The number of colors you use in your color-coding system will vary according to your individual needs. But after choosing the colors you wish to work with, visit your local stationers and buy dots, labels, folders, and pens in those colors. You can use the colors to identify anything from paperwork projects to freezer items and checkbook notations. You'll find it's also a good idea to use a pad of a bright color near the phone. The pad will stand out among the other papers on your desk and make locating messages easier.

4. Make use of clear or translucent accessories.

You'll find that these accessories greatly increase visibility. For instance, if you really don't want to give up writing on little slips of paper, you can organize them by gathering them together and putting them into a clear, zippered case (the kind children use for pencils in a three-ring, loose-leaf notebook).

Whenever I think of translucent accessories (and little slips of paper), I always remember Patrick, an Everything-Out college professor and community activist, who called me in when he'd lost among his papers the annual budget report he'd prepared for the biology department. I understood his concern when we both looked at his piled-up desk.

His in-box, which had long since spilled over, was a mixture of his professorship activities plus papers relating to his involvement with the community health and welfare council and the Leukemia Society. Surrounding his desk on the floor were mounds of books and magazines that had risen to such proportions, Patrick had to step over them whenever he left his desk.

Over and above this disarray—because he hated list-making—were a hundred or so scraps of paper tacked to the wall behind his desk. There were notes covering notes, and everything had become totally nonfunctional. Since Patrick hated to write lists and didn't want to give up his little slips of paper, we took the slips, categorized them as much as possible, and then made use of the clear-zippered cases. We then put the vinyl see-through cases up on his bulletin board, except for one which he carried in his briefcase.

I knew that Patrick would never be happy filing things out of sight, so on our way to finding his misplaced budget I also showed him how to devise a file system using Lucite wall pockets. To set up his new system, we purchased thirty transparent filing pockets and attached them to the walls all around his office. When we were finished, Patrick was literally surrounded by his file system, his avalanche of papers was off his desk, and everything he needed to see was totally visible. This, plus other organizational techniques, helped Patrick use his Everything-Out style productively.

And as we organized his office, we did find his annual budget report so he could present it to the biology department in time.

Instant Summary for an Everything Out

Everything Outs like to leave things out where (hopefully) they can put their hands on them again quickly. When too many things are left out, however, it becomes impossible to find anything. The following approaches will make it possible for the Everything Out to keep things out, but in an organized fashion.

1. Do a desktop survey to determine if you still like and/or use the items you keep there. Remove any that no longer serve a purpose.
2. Follow a basic sorting system for your incoming paperwork so things don't get buried and forgotten in your in-box.
3. Consider desktop organizers that increase your available workspace through divisions or open compartments.
4. Make effective use of wall space for storage and display.
5. Try color coding for quick identification of important information.
6. Look for clear or translucent accessories to give you that feeling of openness and accessibility.

CHAPTER 11

Nothing Out

*I like to keep my desk perfectly clear, but I
still don't feel organized.*

Nothing Outs are the total opposites of Everything Out
individuals. They crave uncluttered and unobstructed
space. They equate a clear surface with a clear mind,
and—until they run into problems—believe they're
being organized when they shove things out of sight.

A perfect example is a folk-artist client who con-
tacted me when she needed help sorting old folk-art
publications—and a nonworking filing system—she'd
kept in her home studio for years. While we sat in her
kitchen talking, prior to tackling the studio, I happened to see her To Do list on which she'd noted the
following items:

Put final coat of shellac on plaque for Gunther.
Check on date for folk-art exhibit at museum.
Handwash knits.
Make soup.
Catch up on laundry.
<u>Clean dirty broiler pan that's in hall closet.</u>

On a second visit to this client we started to deal with
the hundreds of photographs she had not only in her
studio but also under her bed.

"As one of the few remaining people on the maternal
side of my family, I'm keeper of the family pictures,"
she said. "I certainly don't want to display them all. And

yet I feel they're my heritage I need to save for the next generation."

This client's dilemma is a common one, since most Nothing Outs (and Everything Outs) ask me what to do with the photographs they accumulate. Often for Everything Outs an attractive way to organize them is in collage frames on the walls. But this would look too "busy" for Nothing Outs. I usually suggest—as I did with the craftswoman—buying photo albums or sectioned boxes and arranging the photographs in them.

Since Nothing-Out people are also bothered by clutter on their desks, they generally feel claustrophobic when papers are piled there. Consequently, they shove the papers anywhere to avoid looking at them. One of my clients—an English professor who liked all of his papers hidden—had been sticking them in drawers for years. But eventually one of the drawers jammed, and our first task was to get it open and sort through it. The conglomeration was incredible, but as we began to work, he said, "You know, my grad student assistant can't understand how I do things. But really, it's not a mess—it's in a drawer."

Nothing Outs obviously run into trouble when materials they want to conceal become jumbles of disorganization in closets, cabinets, and desks. The day inevitably arrives when drawers don't open and doors jam. Because of this, a Nothing Out's greatest need is a system that operates efficiently while keeping things out of sight.

Are You a Nothing Out?

To find if Nothing Out is one of your organizational styles, take the following quiz. As you answer Never (N), Occasionally (O), or Frequently (F), rate yourself according to the following scale.

Never	Occasionally	Frequently
0 points	1 point	2 points

N   O   F

1. Do you hate to see clutter?
2. Does having a clear desk make you feel as though you're in control?
3. Do you equate a clear surface with a clear mind?
4. Do you shove everything out of sight before guests arrive?
5. Do you prefer to have nothing on your desk but what you need to work with at the moment.
6. Do you buy lots of little boxes and other organizational products that help keep things from view?
7. Do you like writing things down in a notebook?
8. Do you like to put your working materials away after using them?
9. Does putting things back where they belong make you feel as though you're accomplishing something?
10. Do you hide things from sight and then forget that you have them?

Totals:

0–6 points	You're not really a Nothing Out.
7–13 points	You have strong Nothing-Out tendencies.
14–20 points	You're a full-fledged Nothing Out.

Why and When People Are Nothing Outs

There are certain circumstances that, more than anything else, cause people to be Nothing Outs. A prime one is cramped quarters, and individuals who work or live under those circumstances find it difficult to maneuver around normal day-to-day working and living items.

Depending on their individuality they take varying approaches to this problem, and while some of them work and live "with style" when functioning as Nothing Outs, others inadvertently diminish the quality of whatever space they have. Dennis is one of the latter.

As a newly enrolled actuary in a medium-size actuarial firm, Dennis works in a pint-sized office at the rear of the company's suite. Most of the offices, regardless of their size, look inviting and attractive. But Dennis, because of his Nothing-Out style, refuses to be bothered with pictures on the wall, plants in the window, or decorative personal items on shelves. Instead he has covered his open shelves with makeshift mini-blinds to hide the projects he's working on so papers will be out of sight. But even though he achieves this with his folders of client information, government regulations, and various pamphlets and manuals hidden behind the blinds, he creates total chaos for himself as folder after folder is tossed into the "black hole."

Dennis also never throws papers away, so his cabinets of correspondence and forms are nothing short of disasters. Moreover, with everything out of sight and no ambiance anywhere, his office is so cold and stark a colleague who avoids it says, "It's like opening up a freezer and finding nothing there."

Whereas Dennis has cut down on the quality of his space because of his Nothing-Out style, Peggy, a Nothing-Out recreational director of a nursing home, makes her style *and* her space work. Peggy also can't stand clutter. While her solution is also to keep the tops of her desk, worktable, and files clear, for the most part, she neatly and conveniently stores the papers and items she uses in either her corner filing cabinet or low shelves behind louvered doors. And a row of plants in white baskets sits on top of the shelves.

For extra and functional touches Peggy decorates her two-by-four walls with craft items the home's residents make, and in an old china closet she painted to match the walls, she displays a doll collection she brought to the office from her home. The collection has inspired several residents to collect and dress their own dolls. The small cramped space where she functions is a pleasant reflection of who she is and what she has to offer.

Strategies and Techniques for Nothing Outs

Filing

Certainly one strategy Nothing Outs need is a workable filing system so they won't keep papers forever and stuff them haphazardly in cabinets and drawers. Elizabeth, a nutritionist, is quick to admit this.

Elizabeth, who works for a foods corporation and runs a consulting business from her home, inspires confidence. She appears to be so totally in control that when I went to see her, I didn't immediately realize why she was hiring me. But then in a somewhat embarrassed way she opened her closet and desk drawers and showed me her filing and storage system.

"I just can't stand having things lie around when I'm not using them," she said, "so I put them somewhere out of sight to the point when eventually they're so well hidden I can't find them again.

"Just look at these boxes," she sighed as she opened the door to a guest room filled with miscellaneous boxes of every size, shape, and color. "I use them to temporarily file or store things I want to do, take care of, read, whatever. But I'm not getting back to them, and I have forgotten what's where."

I saw why Elizabeth's "system" no longer worked as I looked at the dated labels on the boxes. The first one I saw said "SEPTEMBER," and since it was November at the time I suggested we start going through September as that seemed to be fairly recent. But then Elizabeth said sheepishly, "That doesn't say September of what year."

It was then that I discovered that she had boxes going back for years, many without a year on the box because Elizabeth was always sure that she'd get right back to them. Since she never got back, however, there were things in September boxes for September 1988, 1987, *and* 1986. She also had boxes labeled "ACT I," "ACT II," and "ACT III" for papers she knew required action.

In addition, several cartons of items had been cleared away quickly before company arrived. (On one carton was printed: "From the living room except for one thing.")

To get Elizabeth started on putting things in order we decided on a three-pronged approach:

1. To reduce some of the guilt and pressure she felt whenever she confronted the accumulation, we went through the old boxes one by one to get rid of what we could.
2. To set her up for handling the current things that came in, we implemented the same paper-processing procedures and basic sorting system suggested for Everything Outs. But instead of open areas or containers, we used a *closed* set of stackable drawers labeled:.

INCOMING	TO FILE
OUTGOING	TO READ
	TO DO
	PENDING

3. To comfortably accommodate her new system, she purchased an additional four-drawer filing cabinet.

Admittedly, it took Elizabeth a while to make a complete transition from her old non-system approach because her habit of hiding things in boxes was a long-standing one and resistant to change. But eventually, learning to put things in their proper places enabled her to clear the decks quickly without resorting to sweeping everything into a box where she couldn't find things again for years.

How to File

It has been established that about 80 percent of the papers we receive are never looked at again. So how do you know *what* to file and *where* to put what you need to file?

Easy access to information is the raison d'être for filing, so the first step in setting up a good basic system is categorizing your information and labeling your folders with appropriate generic headings. When you label, start with the broadest categories possible. Later, when the number of papers in a broad category turns the file into a "battle of the bulge," break up that file ("Correspondence," for example) into more than one file in that category—say, "Correspondence A–H," "Correspondence G–N," "Correspondence O–Z" (or whatever labeled subdivision would apply to the generic topic).

When deciding where a new piece of correspondence or information should go, do not ask: "Where should I put this?" Instead ask: "How do I plan to use it?" Determining this will tell you under which category it should be filed. And if you have no plans to use it, be ruthless about throwing it out.

Ideally you should be able to retrieve any paper within a few minutes. If a piece of information could go into two separate categories, select one folder in which to put it, and then place a Xerox copy or a cross-reference sheet in the other folder. Later, if you look for that information in the wrong folder first, the cross-reference sheet will immediately tell you where to find it. An index at the front of your files will serve the same purpose. Color coding can facilitate this process when you use different colored folders or labels for different sections of your files.

Jonathan, a Nothing-Out owner of a small wallpaper and home-decorating shop, calls color coding his "filing shorthand." "My files look like a rainbow," he says, "because—to cite a few examples—I use red folders for orders, yellow folders for supplies, orange for clients, and green for invoices."

As you accumulate new items to file, write a note on how to file them on the items themselves or use Post-It notes. This will give you and your helpers cues for keeping the files in order.

With new material continually going in, your files can get cumbersome, so clear them out on a regular basis. There are several options for doing this.

1. Whenever your folders get too thick to handle easily, weed them out. Hang onto what's active and move everything else to permanent storage or the trash.
2. Go through sections of your files automatically every three months, six months, or a year.
3. Decide ahead of time how long you will keep reports and other types of materials, and mark them with a discard date.
4. Flip through a folder every time you take it out and dispose of the deadwood.

In addition to your basic storage files, there are three other file setups you will probably need. They are currently active-project files, confidential files, and valuable-papers files.

Your active-project files (or working files) are for material you refer to several times a week. Keep them within easy reach in a vertical rack on your desk, a credenza or table, or in a rolling cart. When projects are completed, simply transfer the files to wherever they're to be stored, and set up the cart, table, or rack with whatever new project you have underway. Your confidential files, or personal-interests material, can be kept in your desk side drawers. Your valuable-papers file belongs in a safe-deposit box or fireproof safe. This latter file is for legal documents, securities, insurance policies, and any other papers whose loss would create great inconvenience in case of a fire or other untoward event.

Four final tips for setting up your files:

1. Never have one labeled "Miscellaneous." (How often do you look something up under "Miscellaneous"?)
2. Avoid using paper clips since they tend to slip off easily and catch on other papers.
3. Review regularly notes you've filed from meetings and seminars. Ideas that didn't work before or that were irrelevant at the time may be just what you need now.
4. Retain several inches of play in each file drawer so that it won't jam.

Keeping up with your filing is a weekly job, or more often if it tends to overflow. But if you do it routinely, you'll create a workable system that matches your organizational style and lets you retrieve *what* you need to find *when* you need to find it.

Products

Nothing-Out people tend to buy whatever new organizing product comes on the market as long as the product looks as though it will hide things and help them get their lives, time, and work in order. Five that work well are:

- Day planners/personal planners/organizer books
- Rolltop desks
- Roll-away office carts
- Closed stacking drawers
- Organizers for the inside of drawers/clothes closets/cabinets

1. Day Planners/Personal Planners/Organizer Books

The purpose of these planners or organizer books is to make you focus on your personal and professional priorities as you plan your time and life. And for Nothing Outs their greatest benefit is the way they can help you organize pertinent information in an out-of-sight system.

When making your selection, look for a system that is flexible enough to adapt to your individual situation. This can be achieved by choosing one with premade take-out and fold-in sections and inserts as well as blank pages that accommodate your personal ideas. One of my artistic clients uses the blank pages to design and print up special pages that are divided into To Do sections for her acting career, graphic-design business, and personal life. If you don't like to "go by the book," an alternate to the organizer books—and the ultimate Nothing-Out planner—is a software package that does it all for you on the computer.

Once you start to use a planner, give it time to begin working for you and be sure to keep a duplicate copy of important information. A client of mine lost his, and practically had a nervous breakdown. Also, if there is more than one planner per household, see that the planners are not identical. One woman, a lecturer for a weight-loss organization, picked up her husband's by mistake as she hurried out of the house, What she had for the rest of the day was all of his sales appointments!

2. Rolltop desk

Either a rolltop desk or the kind with a hinged panel that comes down to work on and then flips back up to hide all from view is the perfect desk for a Nothing Out. It can make it possible to do what you want and still live within your style.

Edward was a former history teacher who did oil painting as a hobby, and when he retired from teaching he planned to spend time painting. But when his wife died just before he retired, the house they had lived in for twenty-four years was too large for Edward alone, so he sold the house and the furnishings and started all over again in a spanking-new apartment.

He bought new things for his new home—and set it up to be streamlined. But without his old basement the only place he had for his paints was on the dining-room table.

"I can't leave them out," he told his friends, "and for the two or three hours I'd paint every day, it's too much trouble to put them in a closet and then get them out again when I paint."

His children came up with a solution that they thought he'd like, and for his first retirement Christmas they bought him a handsome rolltop desk, which fits nicely in his living room and hides all of his painting materials when they're not in use.

3. Roll-away Office Cart

Another practical answer for people who don't like to leave anything out is a cart on wheels. These carts provide additional storage space for supplies and files, and when not in use can be kept under a table or in a closet. Carolyn, a Nothing Out whose husband is an electrical contractor, manages the books for him, and for this she uses a file on wheels that fits under a table in her den. She pulls it out when she wants it, does the work she has to do, then rolls it back when she's finished.

4. Closed Stacking Drawers

Closed stacking drawers work the same way as open-stacking desk trays. But obviously they're better for Nothing Outs because they keep papers and supplies out of sight. The drawers can be stacked or arranged side by side and used for forms, stationery, catalogs, office supplies, printed articles, whatever.

Kenneth, an assistant editor on a gourmet magazine, was besieged with publicity releases (and accompanying sample products) for every new food on the market. He needed the releases accessible for a column he wrote, and he also needed a large collection of back copies of food magazines. As a confirmed Nothing Out, Kenneth couldn't tolerate having these things out so he had the people in the mailroom give him large cardboard boxes which he used to toss in—at random—releases, samples, and food magazines. But whenever Kenneth needed information, he had to dig through the boxes.

Our solution for Kenneth was to use:

- Desktop stackable drawers to color code the releases according to the products they represented (breads, soups, pastas, fish, meat, desserts, etc.) with a drawer for each color.
- Magazine boxes that come in corrugated cardboard and imitation wood-grain for the collection of food magazines he wanted to keep.
- A wicker trunk (which the magazine purchased) for his assortment of samples.

As a result, Kenneth now has Nothing-Out storage space, immediate access to whatever he needs, and a handle on where everything is.

5. Organizers for the Inside of Drawers/Clothes Closets/Cabinets

For many people, clothes closets are the last stronghold for stuffing not only their clothes but everything else they want out of sight. But out of sight is not the same as well cared for and easy to find. Too many closet stuffers end up with clothes that get lost or wrinkled, and can never find anything at the moment they want it. Well-organized closets, however, are a must for functioning efficiently. Therefore, a system for storing your clothing is essential, regardless of the size of the space in which you live.

Fortunately, organizing products generally known as space organizers/extenders (that encompass a variety of items from drawer dividers to lazy Susans to entire closet systems) are readily available. Morever, if you need help setting up an entire system, closet-organizing businesses across the country specialize in installations to match individual needs.

Felicia, who imports children's clothing from Europe, is very organized in her small office/showroom. But with her own clothing in her overstuffed closet, she can't find anything.

"Last week I went out and bought a red dress to wear to a party," she said. "Then when I came home, I discovered I had a red dress I'd worn only once that was covered up by a worn-out coat I'd stuck temporarily in the closet. The new dress cost me one hundred dollars that I wouldn't have had to spend."

Felicia's closet was a modern-day version of the famous Fibber McGee's—a legendary character from the golden days of radio, whose closet was so stuffed with junk he couldn't open the closet door without having things spill out all over.

In addition to having more dresses, like the red one, hidden under garments at one end of her closet, Felicia had filled the middle of her closet with a mini-store of mix-and-match blouses, tops, and skirts that she never mixed and matched since whatever she purchased together always got worn together. In the meager space left over she'd jammed her jackets and slacks.

To help Felicia get organized, we took everything out of her closet and first separated wearable clothes from items she no longer wore. Next we sorted her blouses and tops, and put them into one pile. Then we arranged her jackets, skirts, and slacks so each category could be hung back together. When we got to her mix-and-match array, I shuffled them around and asked, "Would you wear this blouse with that skirt?" She enthusiastically answered "Yes," and then added as an afterthought, "I never thought about that before."

Once everything was separated, we made arrangements to install a closet organizer that doubled Felicia's closet space. A floor-to-ceiling vinyl-coated steel section in the middle had grid shelving which allowed her to store and see sweaters and tops. On the right was hanging space for dresses, slacks, and coats. Shelves above accommodated hats and purses, and shelves below held shoes. On the left was a section which had double-decker bars for hanging suits, blouses, and skirts.

When the closet was done, Felicia was thrilled with her new arrangements—and the way her overstuffed closet had changed from a jumble of disorganization to uncluttered and unobstructed space.

"I can't believe we did this," she kept repeating. "But it's wonderful! It works!"

Instant Summary for a Nothing Out

Nothing Outs can easily live a life of illusion, believing that they're well organized and have everything under control while behind closed doors there's chaos. But you can enjoy clear surfaces and still make productive use of your space by following these guidelines:

1. Create *workable* filing systems for both active projects and longer-term storage.
2. Set up a personal planning book or computer program to keep all facets of your life organized in one place.
3. Use a desk with a rolltop/flip-up panel that will hide all from view.
4. Get closed stacking drawers or a cart on wheels for additional storage that can be moved from sight.
5. Redo the insides of drawers, cabinets, and closets with space extenders that compartmentalize open space for more efficient arrangement.

CHAPTER 12

Right Angler

My office looks very neat, but I can never find anything when I need it.

Remember the character Felix Unger, who in Neil Simon's *The Odd Couple* put his underwear on hangers and shoe trees in his bedroom slippers? Felix is the ultimate right angler—so preoccupied with neatness and the way things look that he fails to notice that, all too often, his arrangements make no sense.

It has been said that Right Anglers will even straighten dust balls in corners so the dust balls will look neat. But keeping things lined up with perfectly straight and squared edges does not mean they're organized. Instead, Right Angling encourages (1) saving things you don't need, (2) losing valuable storage or display space, (3) allowing things to "sink roots" in the wrong places, and (4) having a nonfunctional, inefficient system.

It's certainly fine to be neat, of course. But ultimately Right Anglers must understand that it's not enough just to be neat because in their pursuit of neatness they may straighten the wrong things into the wrong places. Then they have a home or office that, even though it looks terrific, can frustrate them—or other people—when they try to locate or retrieve an item.

Lillian, an executive secretary and divorced mother of a son, asked me to help her reorganize her home when another single mother was about to move in with her. We started in Lillian's kitchen, where the pantry *looked* well-ordered and neat. But on the first shelf—in a straight line—was a five-year-old can of cake frosting, stale cereal, a pencil can full of pencils with no points, castor oil, and a dozen used candles three inches long!

Are You a Right Angler?

To find out if Right Angling is one of your organizational styles, take the following quiz. As you answer Never (N), Occasionally (O), or Frequently (F), rate yourself according to the following scale.

Never	*Occasionally*	*Frequently*
0 points	1 point	2 points

N O F

1. Do you feel as though you're getting organized when you straighten things up?
2. Do you like neat piles?
3. Would you rather straighten than clean?
4. Does clutter not bother you as long as it's neat?
5. Do you like arranging things a certain way on tables and shelves?
6. When you are under pressure, does it make you feel better to straighten something?
7. When people move an item out of its place, do you feel compelled to move it back?
8. Does it annoy you when pictures are crooked?
9. Does having to change your systems make you uncomfortable?
10. If something is a real mess, do you tend to stay away from it until you can clear it up totally?

———————

Totals:

0–6 points   You're not really a Right Angler.

7–13 points   You have strong Right-Angler tendencies.

14–20 points   You're a full-fledged Right Angler.

———————

Why and When People Are Right Anglers

There are certain characteristics that typify Right Anglers.

1. They tend to value form over substance.

Rather than thinking of the utility or purpose of items, they concentrate mainly on where items will fit or look nice. Julie, a school-guidance counselor and the mother of four children, is another member of that infamous legion, "Keeper of Family Pictures." A twenty-year accumulation was scattered around her home until she decided to follow my advice to put the photos in albums with loose-leaf plastic sheets. As a Right Angler, however, Julie concentrated on putting the photos in symmetrical arrangements—without any thought whatsoever of chronological order.

Now it disconcerts her family to look through the albums and see photographs of their high school graduations followed by pictures of their birth!

2. They straighten things compulsively as a means of staying in control.

Like David, a client who's a management consultant, Right Anglers find themselves wandering around tidying things up whenever they're worried or frustrated. While waiting to hear from a potential client about a major business proposal, David circles his office, restacking papers, straightening pictures on the wall, and making sure that everything is in its proper place on his desk.

Since he can't do anything about what's really concerning him, the act of arranging what he can arrange gives him an outlet for his nervous energy and the feeling that he is in control of *something*.

3. They may line things up in one area, yet let another area be a disaster.

This is a dead giveaway. Frequently when Right Anglers can't arrange things perfectly, they don't want to touch them at all. Often their reason for this approach—and for being compulsively neat in one area and not neat in another—stems from insufficient time or energy to organize things as they'd like them to be.

Pam, who's the sole proprietor of a communications and graphics firm, has a central open office that is divided into individual workstations for the design staff. The room looks attractive with its Right-Angler style. But the adjacent storage area for supplies is an absolute mess. Since Pam lacks the time to arrange that area exactly as she would like, she prefers to live with the mess rather than straighten it just partway.

4. They like to keep their neat systems as is once they have them in place.

Bert, the director of Tickets for Seniors, an innovative volunteer program that distributes free tickets to people over sixty for activities and events ranging from baseball games to ballet, has shelf after shelf in his office of miscellaneous piles of newspaper articles, program literature, family mementos, pictures, and numerous other assorted items all set up in symmetrical order, or balanced arrangements that correspond in size and shape.

To Bert this "system" was just fine, so that thought of changing any of it was extremely disturbing to him when he suddenly faced a pressing need to rearrange his office. The need arose when Tickets for Seniors began

an expansion program, and as the expansion got underway, Bert required extra space for the fifty part-time
volunteers and increasing load of paperwork now coming into his office.

"But what can I do?" he asked me. "I like the setup
that I have. Everything looks neat as it is, and there's
really no other place to put it."

Working with Bert to arrange for more space was
challenging, to say the least. But we succeeded in creating space. Among other things, we:

1. Sorted through his neat piles and threw out or
   passed on the numerous copies of the same promotional literature and other paperwork and correspondence we found.
2. Set up a scrapbook for all of the newspaper articles
   Bert had collected on Tickets for Seniors so he and
   the entire staff could locate and enjoy them easily
   instead of having to dig clippings out of piles.
3. Created special files for paperwork such as (1)
   voucher validations for tickets to be picked up at
   the door, (2) file updates on members and events,
   and (3) evaluation cards.
4. Separated his personal and professional mail, and
   designated a separate location for the large quantity
   of papers he received in connection with the legal
   affairs he was handling for his widowed mother.

Finally, by making his collection of family mementos
and pictures fit into smaller but still neat spaces, we
managed to preserve some of Bert's original arrangements while providing more organized and accessible
space for incoming material.

Additional Strategies and Techniques for Right Anglers

Right Anglers need sound and viable techniques for
making their style work, so here are more tips to make
Right Anglers' systems look good and make sense.

1. Look for products that will keep things both neat and efficient.

Andy, a chef at a mountain-house resort, has a small office off the kitchen which he uses for planning menus and writing up weekly orders. His Right-Angler office is neat, of course. But he wasn't happy with the open container where he kept his pens and pencils because whenever he wanted a pen or pencil he had to rummage around in the container to find the exact one he wanted. While visiting a friend who's an artist, Andy noticed a container that looked like a small grid. Though it was designed to hold brushes, it was a perfect size for inserting one pen or pencil per slot. Andy immediately bought one—and now has a Right Angler's dream on his desk.

2. Realize that reorganizing jobs do not have to be completely finished in one session.

Since Right Anglers won't touch a job if they can't finish it at one sitting, I have to assure clients that we will finish whatever we start during each session, but that it may take several sessions to complete a large job. In addition, I make sure that we don't leave a mess between sessions that would make them feel too uncomfortable.

Paul, a physical-fitness instructor, was extremely proud of his office library on health-related subjects. All of the volumes were arranged by height—and all exactly one-inch from the edge of the shelves. But when Paul had to locate a specific book, he had an ongoing problem.

To solve it we divided the books into general categories and then by author. But as we worked, we only tackled one shelf at a time, and anything not belonging on that shelf was neatly stacked in the corner until we came to the shelf where it belonged.

3. Periodically examine your needs to see if your systems should be updated.

Because of Right Anglers' reluctance to make changes,

any changes they do make must be the most effective ones for their needs.

I once worked with Jared, a photojournalist who called me in after buying a condo to help figure out where he had sufficient space to set up a small at-home office. We decided on a corner of the dining room, and while checking the room's available storage space, I opened a mahogany chest of drawers and found rubber furniture casters stacked neatly in the velvet-lined silverware drawer. When I asked Jared, "Why are you storing these furniture casters in your silverware drawer?" he peered into the drawer and said, "I really don't have the slightest idea. I guess they've always been there."

As you examine your systems to see if they need to be updated, ask yourself:

1. Do I know where things are and why I put them there?
2. Is everything in a suitable place?
3. Can I find what I'm looking for in three minutes or less?

4. Know that systems can be unorthodox.

There's no one way to organize, so unorthodox systems can be all right as long as they work for you. After her apartment was burglarized, Judi, a commodities broker, decided she didn't want to keep her jewelry together in one spot. Consequently, she had various sized boxes squirreled away all over her home. The problem was there was no rhyme or reason as to what was where, so Judi never knew where to look for the earrings or bracelet she wanted to wear.

When I worked with her, we decided to keep all the boxes. But we put together—and then arranged in separate boxes:.

rings	valuable pieces
watches	• cocktail ring with emeralds
pins	• antique gold lapel pin

bracelets	silver necklaces
pearls	gold necklaces
earrings	costume jewelry
• silver	• black
• gold	• white
• colored	• colored

Now Judi knows exactly where everything is and can find what she wants readily. She's pleased that she *still* has separate boxes so her jewelry isn't kept in one place. Best of all, her arrangements make good sense. And she feels both secure and organized with her unorthodox functional system.

Instant Summary for a Right Angler

Right Anglers are compulsive straighteners. If someone moves something from its "correct" spot, a Right Angler puts it back immediately without even thinking. But keeping things neat doesn't necessarily mean that you're keeping things organized. Systems have to make sense, so if you're a Right Angler:

1. Stay on top of what you are keeping and where you are keeping it to make sure that your arrangements are working for you.
2. Examine your needs carefully and know that it's all right if systems are unorthodox as long as they're functional.
3. Look for products that will keep things both neat and efficient.
4. Realize that the organizing process takes time, but that it can be accomplished without too much upheaval if you tackle a little bit at a time.

CHAPTER 13

Pack Rat

*I hate to get rid of anything that might come
in handy someday.*

One of my clients, a syndicated cartoonist who has done
his strip for twenty years, is a close friend of the comics
editor, and they visit each other's homes. One night the
editor took a letter from his pocket and handed it to
the cartoonist.

"Can you believe this!" the editor asked. "I was clearing out some files this week, and way at the back of one
of them I found this letter asking for a job that you
wrote me twenty years ago.

"I responded with the usual 'We'll keep you on file.'
But I didn't know when I answered you that I'd keep
the letter on file for twenty years! Things have a way of
landing in my files and never getting out."

The comics editor is obviously a Pack Rat of the first
order. When Pack Rats put something somewhere, without really thinking about it, chances are good the item
will stick around for years. Pack Rats are not necessarily
slobs, however. Neither are they collectors in the sense
that they buy and sell their valuables. They just have a
need to hoard and save.

I'll never forget Isabel, a medical assistant who, when
she moved to a new apartment, moved carton after carton of items and keepsakes that once had significance in
her life, but have since become closed chapters. When
she called me in to help find space for the things she'd
moved, we began by sorting through the cartons in her
living room. In the first one we opened was:

- A Valentine Isabel made for her mother when she was so young she couldn't spell "Isabel" except for a sprawling *I*.
- Her tax returns since 1974.
- Her physician grandfather's worn satchel that he'd used when making house calls.
- A certificate for good penmanship she'd received in the fifth grade.
- The bridal headpiece from her marriage.
- An invitation to a New Year's party.
- A broken china demitasse cup.

As Isabel learned through this "awakening," Pack Rats need to become aware that they're in danger of being run out of their homes by their possessions because when every nook and cranny is filled, there really is no place to go. Moreover, it takes time or money (and sometimes both) to take care of their possessions. When too many are saved, Pack Rats who are captives to their belongings can become exhausted from the mental energy used to make decisions about (1) where something is, (2) when they last used it, and (3) whether it needs to be cleaned or fixed.

Are You a Pack Rat?

To find out if Pack Ratting is one of your organizational styles, take the following quiz. As you answer Never (N), Occasionally (O), or Frequently (F), rate yourself according to the following scale.

Never	Occasionally	Frequently
0 points	1 point	2 points

                                                          N O F

1. Do you save things because they might come in handy someday?

2. Do you hesitate to throw something out because someone else might have a use for it?
3. Do you hang onto things because you don't know what else to do with them?
4. Do you feel sentimental about your possessions?
5. Is your home or office running out of storage space?
6. Do people ever wonder why you save as much as you do?
7. Do you keep clothes hoping they will come back in style?
8. Do you feel more secure knowing you have everything you want at hand when you need it?
9. Do you put aside things that are broken with the expectation that you'll get them fixed one day?
10. Do you haunt garage sales and flea markets?

Totals:

0–6 points	You're not really a Pack Rat.
7–13 points	You have strong Pack-Rat tendencies.
14–20 points	You're a full-fledged Pack Rat.

Why People Are Pack Rats

Most Pack Rats don't want things wasted, and this is a major reason for their saving. But there are other reasons, too. The following are four of them.

1. You don't understand that the value of items may change with time.

Pack Rats tend to accumulate things year after year without realizing what they are doing or appearing to note that what seemed essential to keep years ago—for whatever reason—may no longer have the same importance today. That was the problem that confronted Meg, a psychologist who'd filled her office and home with everything she'd ever collected in the various stages of her life.

When she needed to redecorate that office and home and turn an attic storage room into a bedroom for guests, she called me in to help her because the magnitude of clearing out rooms to get ready for the carpenters and painters completely overwhelmed her.

"I've never gotten rid of anything," she admitted ruefully.

I could easily see that when we started working in her office, which was crowded with client files, files of personal research, and stacks of material on what other mental-health professionals were doing. There were also a half dozen shopping bags around. One bag was filled with people's business cards and another contained miscellaneous addresses, each on a scrap of paper that had never been entered in her Rolodex.

She and her husband, a textile designer, have lived in their Victorian house, inherited from her family, for nearly thirty-five years, and since Meg's parents were Pack Rats before her, the condition of her home rivaled her office. In fact, we could scarcely open the door to the attic storage room. And when we tried to clear some space we came across, among other things, Meg's first bicycle, the camera she received for her eighth-grade graduation, a pair of rusty roller skates, essays she wrote in high school, costume jewelry her favorite aunt had given her, and the pearl-trimmed pink sweater she wore to her prom.

Meg's husband is a Pack Rat, too, and as a ham radio hobbyist he had loaded their basement with hundreds of items till it had become a maze. Together the couple had filled up every room until they were both exhausted from thinking of preparing for the painters and deciding what to do with their lifetime of possessions.

2. You think something might come in handy someday.

It's true that something could come in handy if you keep it long enough, and it's equally true that once you get rid of an item you lose the ability to use it. But if you start saving everything, you crowd yourself out of your office or home—and working and living space.

Irene, a nurse who grew up in the Depression, remembers how few household items she had when she got her first apartment, so in her anxiety to keep her children from meeting the same fate she has saved things for them for years. As a result, her basement is crowded with items as diverse as eight toasters that chronicle the advancement in toaster design; three irons with frayed cords; a rocking chair that's missing an arm; boxes of old towels and sheets; and, crammed in the back of the storage space, a manual lawn mower she has kept "in case the kids lack the money to buy a power mower."

In another case Bruce, a printer, hangs on to hobby materials he hasn't used for years because, like Irene, he has the feeling they may come in handy someday. He had once enjoyed carving wooden ducks and doing metalwork for belts and accessories, and while he was involved in those he'd purchased expensive tools and supplies. As time went on, however, Bruce became involved in community projects, and ultimately lost interest in his former hobbies.

"But he won't get rid of *anything*" is his wife's constant lament. "He keeps saying he may get back to these hobbies when he has more time."

3. Your accumulations are your security blankets.

Neal is a chiropractor who specializes in keeping everything so he will have background material on anything he might need to know. He's big on attending conventions, and when I went to his office it appeared he had saved every item he'd ever collected at a conference. One side of his office had two oblong tables he'd covered with skirt-length dark brown felt to match the room's decor. Stashed away under the tables were boxes of convention programs, plus smaller boxes of business cards and name tags from the past fifteen years.

There was also box after box of convention notes and papers that he and other attendees delivered. But never once in his false security did Neal stop to realize many things were outdated because of new developments in his field.

4. You feel guilty about getting rid of things.

Gordon and Jan are partners in a stationery store. In their thirties, they're happily married except for the issue of a collection of vases that fills a mammoth breakfront on one wall of their home.

"The collection was my mother's," says Gordon, "so I feel we have to keep it. But Jan hates those vases with a passion and resents the space that they take up in our small living room.

"She wants me to call in an antiques dealer to take them off our hands. But I can't bring myself to do that. My mother thought she was doing something great when she gave them to us, so I'd feel guilty not keeping them since they meant so much to her."

Nora, an office manager with four children and eight grandchildren, is another person who feels guilty about getting rid of things because she's afraid her family will be hurt if she doesn't keep their gifts. As a result, she has filled a large closet with presents from them. To cite a few items, there are blouses and nightgowns of the wrong size; dusting powder and toilet water (all of a fragrance she's allergic to); earrings for pierced ears (and hers aren't pierced); kitchen utensils she doesn't need; candles of every size and shape; and homemade decorative items the children created in school.

"I keep the closet locked," she admits, "so no one can see where the presents ended up. But I simply can't bear to hurt my family by not keeping what they give me. I always say 'I love it,'—and then I put it away."

Strategies and Techniques for Pack Rats

Reading Matter

Saving up reading matter is an earmark of a Pack Rat (and other styles too), so given the amount of time you have, what is the appropriate mix for reading the daily paper, weekly and monthly magazines, special reports, business books and periodicals, and an occasional novel?

Actually, there's no correct answer. Your own situation must dictate what will work for you. But your reading is of prime importance since it can be vital to know what's happening in your field and in the world in general. As your stack of To Read increases and your time to tackle it decreases, a good place to start is assessing the value of each publication you now receive by asking yourself the following questions.

1. How long have I been receiving this publication?
2. How often do I do anything more than glance at it?
3. What would I miss if I didn't continue receiving it?
4. Of all the reading matter that crosses my desk, what provides the most value for the least amount of time required for reading it?
5. What can I delegate to someone else to summarize for me?
6. Which publications would be beneficial for my people to subscribe to directly?

As you answer these questions, mark the essential publications and cancel your subscriptions to the rest. So you don't miss out on new publications worth adding to your renewals, you may want to subscribe to one new publication on a trial basis each year.

When you've pared down your reading matter to what

you need and want, it's time to put it in order. Start by labeling a container—bin, basket, tray, shelf, or even a drawer in your desk—with "TO READ." Separate the reading material that is technical (i.e., complex matter that will take time to go through) from the nontechnical.

Plan your reading time to take into account this distinction. Generally, your technical reading is best digested during a block of quiet, uninterrupted time because of its depth, detail, and importance. Thus you'll do well to schedule it for specific times when your mental energy is high and you know that you will be relatively free of distractions. On the other hand, nontechnical reading deals with subjects quickly and superficially. It can be glanced through during opportune moments: while on hold on the phone, in doctors' offices, on planes, standing in line, riding in cabs, etc. Both technical and nontechnical reading should continually be prioritized so you will always be aware of what's most important or current. If most of your reading material is nontechnical, you may want to think about taking a rapid reading course.

Give yourself a deadline by which to have each piece of reading completed (for example, a certain number of days or weeks past the publication date). If you don't get through it by deadline time, make yourself discard it. Admittedly, this takes discipline and sometimes, even though you plan to do this, you'll find you're still bogged down with material you intend to read. Chances are good you won't read it, though, if you've gone way past your deadline. Force yourself to get rid of the whole piled-up stack. If you can't go to that extreme, give all material over three months old (except publications that pertain directly to your work) to a paper drive.

Once you get yourself organized to read, you can try a number of techniques. Here are some to get you started:

1. Skim the table of contents. Go directly to the features that you want to read. (If you leaf through the publication, you'll invariably be distracted by other interesting but irrelevant articles.) Read through what you've selected, or just skim again,

highlighting significant areas of interest and making notes in the margin for your secretary to type for review or the files.

2. Stick a Post-It note on the cover to jot down pages for later reading and save the entire issue.

3. Xerox or tear out items of interest and discard the issue.

Important! After making a note to read the article or tearing out the article for reading, make sure you put it back in your To Read pile so you can find it when you want it.

The techniques you choose will naturally depend on the time you've allotted to reading, the various priorities of your projects, the state of your filing system, and the ability of your assistants to help you.

Along with the work-related reading that piles up, many of us have problems with newspapers and magazines also. Daily newspapers typically have a shelf life of one week. Since they're rarely looked at past that time (except perhaps the Sunday paper supplements), you can safely discard a week's worth of daily papers once a week (every Saturday, for example). Should you need something from a major newspaper at a later date, you can usually read it on microfilm in a public library.

Weekly magazines generally have a shelf life of one month. Keep them in a place where they are likely to be read quickly—in the bathroom, on your night table, by the TV, in your briefcase. Most monthly magazines have a one-year shelf life, so go through them at least once a year. (January is a good time to do this before the new year's issues have a chance to pile on top of last year's.) Except for special issues, magazines should be dumped wholesale after clipping. Again, if you need something in the future, public libraries have several years of back issues.

Although clipping can be essential for getting through your reading, you want to avoid what I call the Menu-Clipping Mentality. I'm sure you know people who cut out menus and recipes from newspapers and magazines.

They clip so many of them they have fat folders of menus and recipes, most of which have never been opened or used. The problem is, they look at their collections and feel they're becoming gourmet cooks when they've actually never cooked a single meal.

In no way is cutting something out of the paper the same as cooking it. The idea is to use what you've clipped. So don't clip and save more than you plan to read and use—and once you've cut things out, act on the material within specific time frames.

Other Strategies

I know I can never change a Pack Rat into a non-Pack Rat, and I really wouldn't want to. But, as with the other organizational styles, the negative aspects of this style can be controlled so that Pack Rats can experience more pleasure than pain from their collections. The best way to do this—and this cannot be repeated enough for Pack Rats—is to *regularly* evaluate what you're saving and hoarding, and decide what possessions have value to you today by using the Where to Start—Assessment Exercise recommended for all organizational styles on page 119 in Chapter 9. Specifically, take a walk around your home or office and note:

1. What you currently have.
2. How it is organized and stored.
3. How you maintain those organizational systems.

Next, ask yourself:

1. Do I like what I have?
2. Is each item conveniently placed or stored?
3. Is it easy to put things away?

Many times the basic strategies for all style types are not enough to get Pack Rats moving, however. If you find this is the case the specialized approach of the following strategies will help.

1. Choose carefully the memorabilia you preserve and the means you use for preserving them.

Memories are some of our richest possessions and, to a greater or less degree, nostalgia and returning to pleasant times of the past are delights everyone enjoys. But too much nostalgia in your home or office encourages disorganization and diminishes the pleasure of individual treasures. However, there are some excellent ways to preserve your memories without cluttering up your space. Here are a few examples . . .

- Instead of boxing up and storing your children's outgrown clothes, make a quilt (or have one made) of swatches from special or memorable outfits.
  One administrative assistant, with college-age daughters, cut up the clothes from their school years and by using decoupage, decorated the cornices in her kitchen with the colorful and varied scraps of materials.
- When your space is limited, save only part of your memorabilia.
  Save just the covers of theater programs instead of the entire booklet. Or save just the label from that special New Year's Eve champagne bottle rather than the bottle itself. You'll still have a remembrance of that special time, but you'll be keeping your Pack Ratting under control.

2. Create a Mementos File.

Be selective in your savings by using a Mementos File. This file folder, accordion folder, or box can accommodate only so much, which forces you to evaluate your mementos periodically to see if they're still important to you. This works particularly well for young Pack Rats who might be inclined to squirrel away, without a second thought, everything they've ever created or acquired. If you assist them in going through their collections at the end of every year to save only their favorite papers, artwork, etc., they'll be developing a valuable habit that will help them better manage their belongings in the future.

3. Set up a "Handy Box" or Drawer.

If you're hanging onto things because you think they might come in handy someday, keep your accumulations from getting out of hand by designating a drawer or a box as the "HANDY DRAWER/BOX." When it is full, make yourself take something out before you put something else in.

4. Force yourself to get rid of a certain number of the things you have left.

When clients really need that extra space, I sometimes suggest they get rid of at least one-third of the things they currently have. For some Pack Rats that's too drastic, though, so another alternative is to pick a minimum number of items, and force yourself to get rid of that many things on each shelf and in each drawer in your house.

Bear in mind that clearing things out of your house or office doesn't necessarily mean throwing them away in the garbage, however. Most Pack Rats find it easier to let go if they know that their "valuables" are going to someone else as opposed to the dump. And undoubtedly someone somewhere can make use of your cast-offs.

Hold perennial garage sales. Churches, temples, schools, and hospitals need contributions for their own use or for fairs and fund-raising events. For large items, you can generally find an agency in the Yellow Pages that will pick the items up at your door. If you can't decide to whom to give what, make a list of possibilities on individual slips of paper, toss the slips into a basket, and choose that way.

5. Avoid the "halfway-house" syndrome.

When gathering things together for disposal, make sure you get them all the way out of your house or office within a specified period of time. Pack Rats have a tendency to use garages, basements, and even hallways as a temporary halfway house. If the items are left there too long, they may ultimately return to their original spots, since all too often a Pack Rat is susceptible to second thoughts.

6. Use the "just-moving-in" technique.

As a last ditch measure, try the "just-moving-in" technique. Sometimes things have accumulated for so long that Pack Rats are overwhelmed by feelings of guilt for having let it get to such a point. In those cases I take the Pack Rat out of the house or office and close the door behind us. We then fantasize that they have just been given this new house or office, sight unseen. Whatever they find in there is theirs to do with as they please.

Next I say that whatever mess or unfinished projects they find belonged to the people who were there before them, and therefore are not the clients' fault. With the guilt removed, Pack Rats are in a much better position to make decisions related to their current thinking and style of living. They have a wholly new perspective from which to reorganize.

How to Make a Tendency Toward This Style Work for You

By every standard there is a place in our working and personal lives for saving meaningful links with the past. Some are irreplaceable, so it's fine to allow yourself these connections as long as what you keep does not interfere with your present life. And you *can* weave the past and the present together if you're able to:

1. Find what you have.
2. Use what you have.
3. Enjoy what you have.

I once had a client who was obsessed with cleaning out her basement, which contained the collection of several generations of living. "I know there are hidden treasures there," she said when she hired me. But as she grew more and more obsessed with getting the basement finished, she began to lose sight of why she was doing it in the first place. The job soon became such a huge weight she wanted it over and done with. Her favorite expression for weeks on end was "I'll do such and such—when the basement is organized." But as she grimly concentrated on "just getting done," I reminded her that she was forgetting the whole point of clearing out—her original desire to find, use, and enjoy the many treasures she knew were there.

When she got back on track and relaxed a bit, we discovered, among other things, hundreds of seasonal and holiday items that she was able to use in her house for displays and parties, We also found supplies for doing crafts, a wonderful collection of valuable miniature trains that she and her husband donated to a model-train organization, and, in the mile-high pile of saved-up magazines, turn-of-the-century periodicals that were true collector's items. Eventually this client learned that organizing the basement was a means toward an end—and not an end in itself.

Instant Summary for a Pack Rat

If you're a Pack Rat, getting organized can be difficult. It takes a lot of energy and commitment to part with things that have resided with you for a lifetime. What you have to remind yourself of, though, are the eventual rewards of having more free space, fewer possessions to clean or keep track of, and the feeling of liberation that comes with the knowledge that you're in control of your belongings and not the other way around. You can achieve this if you:

1. Find, use, and enjoy what you want to save.
2. Dispose of or pass on what has outlived its value or usefulness.
3. Refuse to be controlled by stacks of reading material.
4. Teach your children how to evaluate what has meaning to them over the years.
5. Reserve space for new items in your life that serve a function or bring you pleasure.

CHAPTER 14

Total Slob

I can't be bothered with straightening up.

Total Slobs tend to adopt the Pack-Rat style in the way they put items anywhere and seem to see their surrounding world as one giant surface waiting to be covered. But they differ from Pack Rats in the sense that Total Slobs don't intend to hoard and save. Rather, they just accumulate things as they go along. With their inappropriate systems (or with no systems whatsoever) they have great trouble cleaning up and finding things in their rubble. And their habits can make life difficult for the individuals around them.

Are You a Total Slob?

To find out if being a Total Slob is one of your organizational styles, take the following quiz. As you answer Never (N), Occasionally (O), or Frequently (F), rate yourself according to the following scale.

Never	*Occasionally*	*Frequently*
0 points	1 point	2 points

N O F

1. Do you lose things?
2. Do other people complain about your sloppiness?

3. Do you identify with Oscar Madison, the character in *The Odd Couple* who stuffed his brown tie into one of his brown shoes in order to keep track of it?
4. Does it bother you when you're asked to pick up after yourself?
5. Do you agree that "A neat desk is a sign of a sick mind"?
6. Does it seem like too much effort to put things back after you use them?
7. Do you avoid cleaning?
8. Do you have trouble understanding why other people are bothered by a mess?
9. Do you look at a room and not see the clutter?
10. Do you feel as though you have more important and creative things to do with your life than keeping things organized?

_____

Totals:

0–6 points	You're not really a Total Slob.
7–13 points	You have strong Total-Slob tendencies.
14–20 points	You're a full-fledged Total Slob.

Why and When People Are Total Slobs

There are several kinds of Total Slobs, and the roots of their style can stem from a variety of reasons. Here are five major ones.

1. They have insufficient knowledge/skills.

Frequently, Total Slobs had parents who were Total Slobs before them, so they had no other role models from whom to learn. They simply accepted disorganization as a natural way of life.

On the other hand, some Total Slobs never had a chance to learn how to organize because they had mothers or fathers who did everything for them. Through their childhood and teen years their mothers made their beds, cleaned their rooms, and cared for and sorted out their belongings. Thus these youngsters had no experience in taking care of things, managing possessions, and making decisions about their possessions. As a result, they grew up expecting that someone would always take care of whatever they didn't do. And they seldom think about what needs to be done unless they have a forceful partner or coworker.

Kay has been married less than a month to Paul, a law clerk, but she is ready to give up on him for the way he leaves his things everywhere and expects her to put them away. "When he left his muddy running shoes on top of my new microwave, I screamed at him like a fishwife," she said, "and asked him how his mother had brought up such a slob."

"Kay's a nitpicker," Paul declared. "The minute I get home from work she launches into me with '*You* can put your books back on the bookshelf,' '*You* can empty the garbage and trash,' '*You* can hang your clothes in your closet,' '*You* can put your papers away.' I'm as tired of it as she is. My mother was never like that."

2. They lack perception.

Many Total Slobs simply don't see the real condition of their environment because their mind is elsewhere. George is an absentminded mathematics teacher who runs a tutoring service in his Cape Cod home. He is usually concentrating on his students and what he can do to help them, so the only room he is aware of in his house is the room in which he tutors. He wants this room to be casual and informal, so even the most unwilling student will feel at home with him. The room, however, has become so informal that George himself is starting to wonder if, professionally speaking, he needs to do something about it.

The rest of the house which George doesn't "see" is a total disaster zone. When I arrived to work with him, I faced an obstacle course in getting from the front door through the living room to his office. While negotiating my way across the room, I bypassed several pairs of abandoned shoes, some half-eaten bags of potato chips, packages to be taken to the post office, and other miscellaneous items. In his office, unpaid bills were scattered under George's desk. His checkbook was thrown on the floor, and volumes of books on mathematics were stacked up in one corner. A wastebasket overflowed with empty soda cans, and papers to grade occupied one chair. His desk chair had a broken leg, so that was haphazardly shoved aside to make room for the kitchen chair he was using at his desk. As a final touch, a suit to go to the cleaners was hanging on one curtain rod and blocking the light from the window.

3. They are depressed.

Clinical depression (the chronic type) can cause people not to care about the condition of their surroundings.

For example, Ruth, a young working mother, faced with running a household alone and caring for her children with little if any emotional and financial support, became so dispirited and listless that she was completely unable to cope with her secretarial job or with even such a simple chore as cleaning up after a meal. When she'd used every dish and pan that she owned, she resorted to paper plates. And even those plates were often too much to pick up and throw away.

4. They are nonconformists.

Some people believe they're too creative and spontaneous to conform to conventional standards of neatness.

Jennifer, an actress who lives in a littered one-bedroom apartment, got into her chaotic mess because she thinks this is true. With her erratic schedule of acting jobs, looking for acting jobs, and supporting herself in between as a waitress and coat-check girl, she is always in a hurry. Drop-it-wherever-you-finish-with-it is the story of her life.

Once she made a small attempt to separate her living and working space by setting up a part of her living room as a studio area. But this never really worked for her, and the desk she uses to separate the studio area from the rest of the apartment has become a general dumping spot for papers—and everything else. The studio area itself is filled with audition tapes, old scripts, and every issue of *Variety* that has ever come through the door. The entire apartment is in such disarray you'd think a tornado had recently passed through.

"I'm an *artist*," Jennifer said, "and I really do live for my work. I simply don't have the kind of life where I can take time to be neat."

5. They are rebelling against something.

In reacting negatively to authority figures of the past, Total Slobs imprison themselves in a time frame they'd do well to cast aside.

One couple joined together in Total Slobbery both had a strong father figure who never gave up on bringing them up in a Perfectionist-Plus style. They abandoned that style pronto as soon as they got to college, and ten years later it's hard to determine which one is best candidate for "Total Slob of the Year."

Gerald, a salesman, routinely returns from a business trip, dumps his garment bag and attaché case on a vacant chair in his office, and leaves them there until he goes on the road again. His briefcase becomes his workstation, and when he wants a change of ties, he grabs one from the garment bag and switches ties in the office. At home Jeanine, his social-worker wife, has Christmas wrappings (from the previous Christmas) on the seat of a formerly used high chair, and on the tray sits a tarnished silver platter she'd used for Christmas dinner.

Their bedroom is decorated with litter—damp towels from their showers mildew in one corner, discarded clothes are thrown in heaps, and the cast-off newspapers on the floor take the place of area rugs. But Gerald and Jeannine are oblivious to the chaos in which they live.

Strategies and Techniques for Total Slobs

The only permanent way out of chaos is to:

1. Probe your motives for a Total-Slob style.
2. Discard your string of excuses.
3. Accept responsibility for yourself and your environment.

Most important of all, you have to want to live under more optimum conditions. When Total Slobs do this, they can be helped (and help themselves):

1. If they're motivated and persistent.
2. If they do things gradually.
3. If they add a dash of humor to their efforts to be better organized.

Here are some techniques:

1. Simply ask, "What might make things better now?" Rather than "What is the final solution?"

It took a while to get into a maze of disorder, so, understandably, it will take a while to get out of it. But even though nothing will be solved overnight:

- Start thinking now about how things would look if you could wave a magic wand and have your home or office shape up exactly as you'd like it to.
  This fantasy will put you in touch with what's most important to you, and point you in the right direction for beginning your clean-up efforts.

2. Ease into the job.

Even when you know you have to do something about putting things in better order, it's common to hold back because you're concerned that organizing will interfere with your other pursuits. To ease into the job:

- Pick up only a dozen things at a time.
  What do you do on a daily basis in which you can do two thing at once? Perhaps, as an example, watching TV is your way to relax after a day at work. If that's the case, pick up a few things during commercial breaks that hold no interest for you.
- Pick up just ten minutes a day. Most everyone can spare ten minutes.

3. Make getting organized as convenient and simple as possible.

If you're doing a full-scale clean-up in your office, the following rudimentary system should serve your needs:

- Segregate supplies from non-supplies.
  Supplies are anything that hasn't been used as yet in the creation of a product, such as blank paper, pens, paper clips, empty boxes, and unused folders. Store them together in a place that's easy to get to.
- Take all printed or written material (notes you've written, letters, magazines, newspapers, books) and divide them into only three categories:

    1. To File—leave them on the floor.
    2. To Read—put in a chair.
    3. To Do—put on your desk.

In your home, try the following tips:

- Place a clothes hamper near the spot where you undress.

- Put the clothes that you take off (that don't go into the hamper) all in one place.

  If you can't make it to closets and drawers with the clothes, leave them all in one chair. Then when you get to tidying up, they will be in one spot. Try to clear off the chair at least every few days or when the pile topples over onto the floor.

- Set a clear-glass fishbowl with a wide mouth on top of your dresser or bedside table and confine its use to the jewelry you wore during the day, keys, change, your watch, and other miscellaneous items that came home in pockets or purses.

  The clear bowl will enable you to see what's in there, and the wide opening at the top will make it easy to pull out what you want.

4. Motivate yourself with rewards and incentives.

Rewarding yourself is a technique that works in adulthood as well as in childhood, so two strategies that will help—as they've helped many Total Slobs—are (1) rewarding yourself along the way as you see some progress, and (2) planning something special to work toward.

A sculptor whom I counseled had a passion for unique wooden earrings, so the best reward for this woman was buying herself a new pair every time she could see she was moving ahead in her order-out-of-chaos project. Her ultimate reward, however, was planning a party for her friends because, for as long as she'd had an apartment, she'd wanted to have people over. "But my place was such a mess," she said, "I never felt I could do it."

Now as she's putting things into shape she knows that she can do it, and she's inspired to continue doing it to get ready for the party. "I still occasionally balk at picking up," she admits, "and when that happens, I cater to myself and let things go to the next day. But I don't let things go day after day because I've learned what happens: it's a lot harder later on!"

Instant Summary for a Total Slob

Total Slobs, who are sometimes Pack Rats, too, are the complete opposites of Right Anglers. They have a high tolerance for mess and not much experience in straightening it out. But even Total Slobs can become organized by using these guidelines:

1. Accept responsibility for yourself and your environment.
2. Work gradually at improving things.
3. Adopt systems that are convenient and simple.
4. Motivate yourself with rewards and incentives.

CHAPTER 15

If Two Different Styles Collide

I'm comfortable doing things my way, and it irritates me when other people want to do them differently.

Glen, a Perfectionist-Plus tax consultant, is as punctual as a clock. But Saul, a Hopper and fellow consultant who works in a branch office of Glen's firm, constantly loses track of time and is late for every appointment. For months this conflict in organizational styles made Glen's blood pressure rise, until he decided the best approach was (1) to recognize that Saul, from his point of view, had little regard for time, and (2) to make a mental compromise to meet their styles halfway.

Glen's compromise? Whenever they scheduled an appointment, he told Saul that they'd meet an hour earlier than he expected Saul to arrive. On *his* calendar, Glen scheduled the appointment for an hour later than he told Saul. As a result, when Saul dashed in late, he wasn't really late at all. And Glen had a productive hour to get things done at his desk—without becoming irritated as he kept his eye on the clock.

Since all of us live and work with others, the odds are good that, like Glen and Saul, we'll be involved at work or at home with persons whose styles collide with ours. But even though it's human to believe our style is the one that's right, we have to consider other people's styles too, and learn how to make adjustments when two styles clash.

Fortunately Glen had a good sense of humor and, at least in this case, enough flexibility to cope with Saul's organizational style. But adjusting to the styles of others is especially trying for persons with the more inflexible styles, who think other people should do things exactly as they do them. This expectation is unrealistic and causes much tension and stress.

Minimizing Tension and Stress

Fortunately, there are ways to minimize tension and stress.

1. Take someone else's point of view seriously.

Learn to really listen even if it's uncomfortable. You may hear something surprising that will help you understand the problem better. To make sure you hear the message correctly, stop what you've doing and repeat what you've heard. Pay attention to body language as well as words.

2. When possible, compromise or barter.

Unless one person is required to abide by the opinion of the other, some sort of compromise is in order. The best way to compromise is to start with what you would like ideally and what the other person would like ideally. Then look at the flip side and consider the minimum conditions both of you could accept. Think creatively and look for a solution somewhere in between the minimum and ideal. Be certain that both of you agree that enough of your needs are being met to be fair.

An alternative solution is to barter—to make an even trade or exchange. (For example, "I'll let you do x if you'll let me do y.") In this way, each person gets to keep his/her style's approach intact for at least some of the time.

3. Develop a sense of humor.

Constant tensions can certainly get you down, but circumstances are usually not terrible unless you think they are. Attitude plays a big part in coping with style clashes, so try altering your perspective to see a bright side, wherever that may be. A new attitude may give you more positive energy to cope with the situation. It may also help you recognize that other persons are not usually trying to irritate you with their style differences even if that seems to be the case.

4. Keep the lines of communication open.

Remember, as long as you're talking to someone, there's a chance of resolving differences. It takes skill and determination to negotiate successfully, but almost any problem can be worked out if you're sufficiently motivated. Perhaps invite a third party to moderate the discussion. But make sure the third party is clearly objective and someone whom you both respect.

Making Adjustments When Different Styles Clash

1. Perfectionist Plus vs. Allergic to Detail

Marshall and Lee, the owners of a shoe-store chain, had the potential for a perfect partnership—complementing each other as they did with their two different styles. But first they needed to understand and work through the problems that their opposing styles created.

When they began their partnership, they recognized that each partner had his own special strengths. But methodical Marshall, who wanted everything so perfect he'd move price stickers to exact spots in the upper left-hand corners of boxes, soon felt frustrated with Lee's disorganized manner. When Lee, because of his scrambled paperwork, would either overbuy or forget to buy the stock they needed, Marshall would worry constantly about their nonfunctioning office systems.

As time went on, the partners began to get on each other's nerves. Marshall was constantly annoyed at Lee's refusal to do something as simple as empty his own wastebasket when it started to overflow, and Lee discovered to his dismay that Marshall was going behind his back and redoing the windows Lee had just finished dressing.

When I came in, I suggested that the partners talk about their problems over breakfast on a Saturday morning. This would get them away from the pressures and interruptions at their warehouse office, and enable them to relax and consider things from a different perspective. I accompanied them for that first meeting and proposed that they slow down for a minute and ask each other: "What is your objection to what I'm doing?"

"Marshall thinks that everything should work the way he wants it to work," Lee said immediately. "He doesn't understand that I have my own way of getting things done."

"But I think my way is better," asserted Marshall. "I'm older and have more experience than you do."

"Then why did you want me as a partner?" Lee retorted.

"Because you have an eye for design and marketing strategy that's much fresher than mine," Marshall answered. "But you don't pay enough attention to what really makes the wheels turn around here. Your idea of filing is to commit every order to memory, and then just toss the written confirmation into the garbage—which might even work if you *had* a memory."

"Now wait a minute," countered Lee. "Maybe I don't think it's necessary to spend three whole days double-checking figures when I could be meeting salesmen and getting around to the branch stores. But—"

I interrupted at this point. "Are you two talking about *what* you do or the *way* you're doing it?"

Marshall sat back to consider this. "I think Lee is right about the need to meet salesmen and visit the stores," he acknowledged. "What I'm objecting to is the fact that he moves so fast and in such an undisciplined fashion, I can't document what he's doing. I feel out of control."

"But your way takes so much time," Lee complained. "I'd never get out of the office."

Marshall, half smiling, then asked Lee, "Have you ever actually tried my system?" Then the two of them laughed out loud at the obvious answer—and the image of Lee racing away from even the mention of paperwork.

I suggested that perhaps now was the time for Lee to implement some simple, basic approaches that would make life easier for Marshall. But I also reminded Marshall that Lee's preference was for systems that were not too time-consuming.

With my assistance the two of them came up with the following innovations for Lee:

- A wall-mounted scheduling board to record Lee's appointments and buying trips.
- A set of loose-leaf notebooks to hold numbered order copies.
- Order forms for each vendor, to be kept in an alphabetized file.
- A separate color-coded file for letters of cancellation.
- Magazine boxes to hold supplier catalogues.
- Regularly scheduled blocks of time to review together paperwork, questions, and problems.

With Lee's compromise in order, Marshall agreed for his part to go along with Lee's way of dressing the windows, even though he would have preferred them to be done differently.

Obviously the partners' attitudinal changes didn't come overnight—this can never be expected in any style clash. But Marshall and Lee initiated a healthy dialogue, and decided as a result to continue their Saturday breakfasts so they would have a regularly scheduled opportunity to settle differences and work on future plans.

I recommended that at every meeting they take turns asking the other, "How can I help you make better use of your time?" The give-and-take of this communicational technique would show both of them:

1. Whether or not they were beginning to get in each other's way again.
2. Whether one of them needed special assistance.

Lee's sense of humor has seen them through a great many situations, and now, instead of growing impatient, Lee has learned to laugh at Marshall's compulsiveness—and even joke that when everyone goes home, Marshall stays late to dust the boxes.

Despite the strides they're making, however, in merging their Perfectionist-Plus and Allergic-to-Detail styles, both are aware that some things are never going to change. At the opening of their newest store, for example, Marshall was dismayed to find a back corner where the new paint was slightly chipped and insisted on calling the painters back in. And Lee will never remember to empty his wastebasket, so Marshall has taken it upon himself to do that chore each day. But Marshall and Lee are learning and adapting—and their business is becoming successful in spite of (or maybe because of) their two different styles.

Strategies that work in a situation such as Marshall and Lee's are:

1. Talk about your problems at a time when you can both relax and consider them from the best possible perspective.
2. Ask "What is your objection to what I'm doing?"
3. Define minimum conditions that both styles are willing to accept. Make clear how strongly you feel so the other person can better understand what you want. (For example, rank your feelings on a scale of 1 to 10.) Then work out a compromise.
4. Periodically ask, "How can I help you make better use of your time?"
5. Realize that some things may never change.

2. Right Angler vs. Everything Out

Laurie and Brad live in a small suburban home, and were always at odds about their different approaches to organization. As a Right Angler, Laurie was preoccupied with the way things look, and to her, good organization meant keeping things straightened up.

But Brad, as an Everything Out, didn't want to spend his time putting things back where they belonged, and after a day in his high-pressured investment business he saw his home as a refuge where he could unwind and let everything fall wherever. From his point of view, he couldn't care less whether the house looked straightened.

Since Laurie worked at home as a newsletter editor, however, she felt the need to keep the house in order because if she ignored the demands of housekeeping, the results of her inattention surrounded her—and she couldn't tolerate that.

"Brad constantly dumps everything into my neatness," she said in disgust. "The first thing he does after work is drop his briefcase, newspaper, and gym bag on the dining room table and the floor right by it. Then he heads upstairs to change his clothes. I like to keep the table clear, so I take his things off the table and pile them neatly on a corner chair."

Later, when Brad comes downstairs, he's horrified at the straightened-up pile and angry at Laurie's interference. "Why can't you leave my things alone?"

"And why do you drop things all over?"

The first thing I did in working with this couple was to ask them to switch roles and try to argue from the other person's point of view. Brad became the Right Angler who felt compelled to keep everything straightened, and Laurie was the Everything Out who saw no harm in having things lie around. Naturally, it was difficult for them to comprehend completely the rationale of the other style. But at least they made a start toward seeing how the other person felt to have wishes ignored and needs criticized.

The second thing we did was to clarify exactly what wasn't working in Brad and Laurie's attempts to get each other to abide by their separate points of view. Brad told Laurie that her nagging only made him less responsive to her requests, and that he really disliked her habit of stacking up his belongings to make them look neat.

"But where does that leave me?" she asked. "What can I do to keep this place under control if you won't pay any attention to what I say?"

Our third approach was to work out a major compromise that would meet the needs of (1) Brad's desire for space that could be messed up, and (2) Laurie's wish for space that could be kept neat.

As we discussed alternatives, I learned that Brad had a corner of their bedroom with a desk and filing cabinet that he used for handling household paperwork—which Laurie straightened up every day. They agreed that if Brad would collect his mess from wherever it had fallen during the day and then consolidate and confine it to his corner in the bedroom at the end of every evening, Laurie wouldn't touch it. In fact, Laurie even promised to pretend that Brad's corner was not part of the bedroom.

With the agreement in force, the shared areas in the home (including the dining room) were straightened up each day. But Brad's own area remained just the way he liked it.

Strategies that can work for a situation such as Laurie and Brad's are:

1. Switch roles to see how it feels to have another organizational style.
2. Clarify what isn't working in your attempts to resolve the situation. For example, see if either of you consistently reacts with expressions of disgust or outrage that automatically puts the other person on the defensive and makes it difficult to discuss things objectively.
3. Work out a compromise that, if possible, includes

a separate and private area for each person to organize as he/she sees fit.
4. Aim for a "win-win" situation. Both of you should
be able to emerge feeling okay about what has
transpired.

As people with different space styles at home work
out a style clash, they must keep in mind that the strategies call for a basic understanding of the three points
that follow if they are to succeed:

1. All of us should have at least one place that is
entirely our own to do with as we please as long
as the conditions pose no health hazard.
2. The appearance of a home reflects the values of
the people who live there. Public areas need to be
maintained at least at a minimum level that satisfies
all residents.
3. In times of crises—accelerated demands, illness,
and special projects—people tend to fall down on
their end of the bargain. This calls for patience plus
a mutual understanding of when regular systems
will be resumed.

How to Manage Your Staff's Time Styles

Managing your staff's time styles—and succeeding—
is a challenging problem, as Jason, who heads the public-
relations department in a large corporation, discovered.
Jason is in charge of a staff of four. But, like Marshall,
he's a Perfectionist Plus. He expects the team that's
under him to perform exactly as he does and to meet
the schedule he sets up for press releases, pamphlets,
speech writing, special events, and all the other activities
that promote a favorable image for the corporation. His
staff, however (though the people mean well), represent
four opposing styles.

Kent is second in command and responsible for implementing the programs the team creates. But Kent is such

a Fence Sitter that before he starts working on anything, he spends hours that run into days weighing every pro and con that could possibly occur.

Tracy was hired to arrange special events and maintain good media contacts, and she loves the overall glamour of that phase of her job. But as an Allergic to Detail, she too often misses a key detail in setting up an event. This causes rough spots now and then, and naturally disturbs Jason.

Steve is in charge of press releases and writing pamphlets and brochures. But Steve is an all-out Hopper and never completes one of his tasks (as Jason would like him to) before Hopping on to something else.

Alyce is the newest and youngest staff member, and while she is in training, it's her job to maintain files of material about the corporation, clip appropriate newspaper and magazine articles, and do research for proposed pieces. Alyce has Cliff Hanging tendencies, though, so she puts off the research which she likes least, and in not completing that on time, she often holds up the entire team.

Since Jason really likes many of his staff's qualifications, he has no desire to fire anyone. But in order to guide the team effectively and motivate people to perform more to his liking, he must recognize each person's individual organizational style and then apply management methods that will help each person work with the style, not against it.

Some strategies that Jason can use for managing his staff's time styles are:

1. For Kent, the Fence Sitter

- Set up a time line so he will always be aware of the planned kickoff dates for upcoming publicity programs. Mark deadlines on the time line for deciding on an approach for each program.
- Make sure he knows what facts and figures are needed, so he won't waste time worrying if he has enough information.

• Check on his activities periodically and reassure him as progress is made.

2. For Tracy, the Allergic to Detail

• Help her plan a step-by-step schedule so no key details for events will get lost in the cracks. Set it up as simply as possible because she will skim anything complex.
• Suggest that whenever she starts working on an event, she set up an expandable file to be kept solely for that event and for every paper pertaining to it. Encourage her to look at the file regularly.
• If possible, assign her an excellent support person who will help her keep track of the details.

3. For Steve, the Hopper

• Limit the number of assignments he's involved in at any one time—maybe two or three are sufficient. But refrain from insisting that he stick to just one assignment until it's completed or he'll become bored.
• Encourage him to create a schedule for himself that takes advantage of his changing energy levels and allows for smooth transition from one activity to the next.
• Give him an office or work space that is free of as many distractions as possible so he won't become sidetracked.

4. For Alyce, the Cliff Hanger

• Help her establish the last possible deadline for getting her research material to staff members. Say, "If we don't have this by March 10, we're dead."
• Suggest she write down dates so there's no misunderstanding about when material is due. Stress that you expect the due dates to be met. Also say, "If there's going to be any problem meeting these dead-

lines, I expect to be notified as early as possible so we don't have a crisis on our hands.''

- Accept her last-minute flurry of activity as long as deadlines are met and her assignments are done satisfactorily.

The foregoing strategies will help Jason manage his staff of four. But Jason in turn has a boss over him—an executive vice-president—who needs to apply the management methods that will help *Jason* perform at his best. Thus the executive vice-president needs to take into account Jason's Perfectionist-Plus time style:

- See that Jason doesn't put in too much overtime and end up suffering from burnout. Working long hours will not be necessary for Jason if he has an adequate, appropriately trained, and well-utilized staff under him.
- Be careful about swamping Jason with work since Jason probably says yes to any request for his time.
- Compare his priorities to Jason's to make sure Jason is putting emphasis on the correct projects.

How to Manage Your Staff's Space Styles

Managing your staff's different space styles can be a sensitive area because a sloppy office may or may not correlate with a person's performance. On occasion, your problem with a subordinate's space organization may be your personal reaction to a sloppy office style. For example, if you are a Nothing Out, your response to an Everything Out's office organization may be just a reflection of your taste and preferences rather than a measure of that person's competence on the job. When this is the case, you pretty much need to let your staff go with their own space styles and as their manager simply help them keep their styles under control.

To decide whether to leave your staff alone or to give them some help, determine whether their individual work areas are causing difficulties for them, your department, or the company as a whole. Ask yourself the following questions:

1. Are any of my people misplacing or losing things with annoying frequency?
2. Are they causing complaints from others who have to use or share the same work space?
3. Are they giving my department a bad image because of the condition of their office?

If the answer to any of these questions is yes, there are several things you can do.

• Consider whether the construction of the work space or office itself is a contributing factor.

    Cramped quarters, poor lighting, inadequate or inappropriate equipment, can all create problems. Perhaps improvements can be made in some of these areas. If nothing can be done, however, your staff may need assistance in adjusting to the working conditions.

• See if the individual's processing systems are at fault.

    Staff members who don't know how to effectively handle their paperwork or retrieve material from the files will have work areas that reflect this. Some simple educational procedures can solve this.

• Assess the person's style of space management to figure out how that person's approach can be controlled so it will come more into line with company policy.

    For instance, all styles, but particularly Pack Rats, should be encouraged to go through their papers, books, and materials every few months to weed out what's no longer needed or functional. Some companies devote an entire working day to this at least once a year.

    Nothing Outs and Right Anglers usually don't have an image problem with their office, but managers need to remind them to check their piles and drawers occasionally to make sure their systems are functional. Generally you'll find it's the Everything Outs and Total Slobs who generate the most complaints in offices, and when you manage them you may be called upon to exercise the most control. While doing this, however, recognize that Everything Outs and Total Slobs will never turn into Nothing Outs and Right Anglers. They'll rebel at any attempts to maneuver them in that direction. What you can do to help them most is to implement the simple systems that will keep things manageable while still more or less in view.

As you live and work with others whose styles collide with yours, you'll find that those with different organizational styles will probably never see eye to eye in every situation. But they can find workable compromises that all persons involved can live with.

And as Glen and Saul, Marshall and Lee, Laurie and Brad, and Jason and his staff discovered, they can co-exist amicably if they respect each other's opposite needs and individual styles.

CHAPTER 16

Special Situations—When You Can't Go with Your Style

I was doing fine, but then something happened.

No matter what your style is—and regardless of how well it works—you'll run into situations at times when (for at least a temporary period) you can't go with that style. The situations that cause this come packaged in many ways. But the three that are the most prevalent are:

1. You find yourself in an environment where you don't have the flexibility to conduct yourself exactly as you'd like to.
2. You have to deal with extra pressure.
3. You're faced with a major crisis in your work or personal life.

These situations are bound to affect every organizational style. Here's how they were met and handled by an Everything Out, a Cliff Hanger, and a Perfectionist Plus.

1. You find yourself in an environment where you don't have the flexibility to conduct yourself exactly as you'd like to.

Murray, a hardworking senior manager for a business-machine company, is an Everything Out who had great problems when his longtime secretary had to leave. His company in turn had problems with him, since Murray was unable to keep anyone the company hired for replacements.

The former secretary, like Murray, had been an Everything Out, so working amid Murray's clutter never bothered her. She'd always anticipated his needs and literally read his mind. But new secretaries couldn't take his demands and incomprehensible systems, so three had left in a matter of weeks for a less exhausting and confusing job.

By the time his superiors called me in to talk with Murray, everyone was impatient with his "secretarial revolving door."

"But you wouldn't believe what they send me," he said. "The people can't keep track of papers, and they don't comprehend what I want. Yet I certainly don't see why I need to change simply because a secretary doesn't understand the systems I've used for years.

"If I had my own business," he went on, "I'd have the flexibility to interview and hire until I found the right person. But since I'm part of a company, I have to take what they give me. I really don't know what I'm supposed to do next."

For Murray, the solution—if he wanted to keep his job—was learning to work in an environment where he didn't have the flexibility to go with his style completely and conduct himself exactly as he always had. To help him adjust in the best way he could manage, we talked about strategies for making his Everything-Out style as functional as possible, while emphasizing his need for approaches that could be easily understood and used by a new secretary. We came up with the following compromises and solutions:

- The establishment of regular meetings with his secretary to keep her updated on current business.
- An in-progress file in a vertical rack on his desk for accounts that he was reviewing. At every meeting he would let the secretary know what files could be found there.

- A coherent alphabetized filing system for all other papers not in progress.
- A bright red folder for messages and high-priority mail brought in by the secretary, so those items wouldn't get lost among the other papers on his desk.
- A coded priority system (see below) for handling assignment changes and emergencies so the secretary wouldn't have to guess which items were most critical.

Important	Do before week is out.
Urgent	Do before day is out.
Rush	Drop everything to do this now.

I suggested that Murray also train himself to refrain from marking everything "Rush" and "Urgent" by first saying to his secretary, "I need a rush job done. Let's look at your workload for today to see what can be put on the back burner temporarily so this job can be handled."

Through these approaches Murray was able to retain certain aspects of his casual Everything-Out style (like an overfilled desktop) even though he couldn't go with it all the way because of the need to accommodate a new secretary. But by altering his style and behavior somewhat, Murray and his latest secretary now function as a team.

If you find yourself in a less flexible environment than you'd like:

- Determine what restrictions and limits are being placed on the expression of your natural style.
- Acknowledge these limits and see how you can work within them to achieve your goals.
- Try to be patient and open-minded.
- Think creatively and design new approaches that will allow you to do the job as comfortably as possible.

2. You have to deal with extra pressure.

Elaine, a twenty-nine-year old nuclear engineer who's also completing a doctorate in mechanical engineering, used to be able to function well in a Cliff-Hanger style. She always relied on just getting by and finding time to take care of things when something went wrong at work or home in the eleventh hour.

But when she had a baby, the extra pressure in her life played havoc with her Cliff-Hanger style, since she'd never considered that she'd no longer have moments to spare because of taking care of her four-month-old son before and after she went to work and he went to a day-care center.

At work Elaine is employed as a project manager at a national research laboratory, and her job is to study atomic-reactor accidents like Three Mile Island and Chernobyl in order to prevent others like them. She took three months' maternity leave. But she soon found, on returning to work, that the three-pronged pressure of a demanding job, a doctoral committee setting a date for her oral exam, and the care of her infant made her feel that day by day she was sliding toward the brink of disaster. Her Cliff-Hanger style was falling apart when she called me in.

"Just this week I was forced to postpone a major presentation," she said, "because I waited till Sunday, the day before the presentation, to plot my data on the computer—and then the computer went down. With no one available to fix it on a weekend and no other resources available to use, I was stuck.

"The previous week I also ran into serious trouble," she added, "because, while under pressure to meet another deadline, I was notified by my boss that I'd missed a critical detail in the design of a fuel container which would result in expensive reconstruction.

"At home I have nightmares about not being prepared to take my doctoral exam, and I feel my home life is suffering, too, because when I want to spend the evening with my husband and son, I'm torn between my wish to be with them and the need to work and study in order to stay ahead of the eight ball."

All Cliff Hangers during times of extra pressure need to put more structure into their lives and plan their time carefully. For Elaine we set up the following weekday and weekend schedules. This will help her keep a balance between the important areas of her life and still be flexible enough to accommodate special needs in any one area while her extra pressure is so intense.

Weekday Schedule

6:00–7:15	Get up one hour ahead of everyone else in order to take advantage of quiet time to study for orals and eat breakfast.
7:15–7:30	Get son dressed for day care. Husband will feed him and then drop him off on his way to work.
7:30–8:00	Dress and get ready to go to work.
8:00–8:30	Drive to work and start day.

WORK

5:30–5:45	Drive to day-care center to pick up son.
5:45–6:00	Drive home.
6:00–6:30	Feed and play with son.
6:30–7:00	Prepare dinner while son is in playpen.
7:00–7:30	Eat dinner and discuss day with husband, who has just arrived home.
7:30–8:00	Clean up from dinner.
8:00–8:30	Family time. Then bathe and put baby to bed on alternate-night schedule with husband.
8:30–11:00	Take care of household chores or work on lab projects that are coming due.
11:00–12:00	Personal time for exercise, reading, TV, or time with husband.
12:00–6:00	Sleep.

Weekend Schedule

Instead of planning the weekend hour by hour, we simply divided each day into three time slots: morning, afternoon, and evening. Evenings were reserved for social or family activities. For the daytime hours—since Elaine's schedule was currently more demanding than her husband's—we scheduled one morning and one afternoon slot for Elaine's studying and work-related activities, and her husband took the other morning slot as personal time. The remaining afternoon time slot was to be used for family outings.

In addition to the weekday and weekend scheduling, we came up with two ideas for Elaine to use at work to help prevent the occurrence of last-minute glitches like those she had suffered through.

1. Plot or document data as soon as it is generated. This will help avoid the mad scramble to find papers and turn rough sketches into presentation-quality material right before it is due.
2. Schedule weekly meetings to share data. This type of peer review will encourage questions and dialogue that may alert her to details that were missing in time to avoid a crisis.

If you have to deal with extra pressure:

- Consciously structure your time more carefully to make sure all the bases are covered.
- Be prepared for Murphy's Law.
- Try to stay healthy and keep your body in good shape to deal with the added stress.
- Enlist the support of others to help out whenever they can.
- If activity becomes especially frenzied, sit back and make sure that you still have the situation in perspective.

3. You're faced with a major crisis in your work or personal life.

Everyone knows that a lifetime brings personal and emotional crises, but the workplace also brings many organizational crises, and when you're required to meet them your style can have its wings clipped. Take the case of Roger, a Perfectionist-Plus interior designer who had to sacrifice his perfectionistic standards and make the best of a bad situation while dealing with a work-related crisis.

It all began for Roger when he was hired to design new quarters for a mail-order house that specialized in selling designer sports clothing and equipment. The company's business had mushroomed, and though it previously had published only spring and summer catalogs, it was now in a position to put out a winter one as well. To do this the company needed to increase staff size and move to larger quarters when the lease on their current property was up on July 1.

When Roger took the job he covered all bases by (1) carefully researching the company's needs; (2) designing an effective layout; (3) ordering elegant but functional furniture that would facilitate the traffic and work flow from information assembly and creative artwork through to production and shipping; and (4) working toward the time schedule the company had given him.

Second week in June	Move from old quarters to new quarters.
July 5	Have new plant operational so production work on winter catalog can proceed without delay.
Labor Day Weekend	Have everything in order for formal grand opening party at new headquarters.
September 5	Release Winter catalog.

As Roger went over the details again and again, he thought he had everything covered. But the week before the company was scheduled to move, the shippers at the furniture factory went on strike and the mail-order house was forced to move into the new building with its old, instead of new, furniture. Because the staff had been increased to get out the new catalog, there was insufficient furniture to accommodate the additional people. But since the catalog-release date was September 5, production had to go on.

Roger was naturally upset by this turn of events because as a Perfectionist Plus he wanted everything to fall in line. Consequently, it was difficult for him to be comfortable even thinking of a makeshift solution. But he did what any good interior designer would do, and totally sacrificed his Perfectionist-Plus standards to resolve the problem.

Working within the confines of a new tight budget, he arranged for the purchase of material including sawhorses, doors, and thick plywood for the construction of additional desks and worktables. He rented extra chairs and bought old file cabinets from a surplus furniture store that could be retained later for dead-file storage. Since the light fixtures could not be installed until the furniture was placed, he also brought in extension cords for temporary lighting where it was needed.

These arrangements made it possible to accommodate the additional staff and proceed with the winter catalog production. But when that was in order, Roger was immediately faced with a new crisis. He learned that the company planned to go ahead with its scheduled grand opening party on the Friday before Labor Day.

"I'm not a miracle worker," he exclaimed. "There's no way to get this place ready in time. If the furniture doesn't arrive, we're left with all of these makeshift pieces."

Roger was completely thrown by the thought of party guests looking at the results of his design job. But the company was adamant about having the grand opening at the scheduled time and in the scheduled place rather than a rented spot. In June it had sent out promotional literature to customers and the media about the upcoming new catalog and the formal grand opening party to be held at their brand new headquarters. Both the company's image and a great deal of money was already invested in throwing this party.

At the time all of this was going on, I was consulting on a different project at the mail-order house. I was called in for a meeting with Roger—and the other people involved—to come up with some kind of solution to make the best of what the company now had.

While we all put our heads together one of the staffers casually remarked that working in that makeshift environment was like being in a circus. With that remark came the idea to change the event from a formal buffet to a theme party with a circus as the theme. This seemed like an acceptable solution for presenting the building in its half-finished state, so we went ahead and printed up invitations saying "Come to the Circus." To go in with the circus theme, we had streamers and balloons, candy apples and popcorn, and clowns and magicians. We even had the children of staff members dress in circus attire to distribute copies of the catalog.

Although Roger needed help in dealing with the party crisis, the experience did show him some general techniques for handling crises that even a Perfectionist Plus could use successfully.

If you have to handle a crisis:

- Pause to survey the situation. Ask yourself, "Is this really a crisis, or am I just reacting to it as though it were?"
- Retain your composure. People who look to you for guidance will be reassured, and will be less likely to run off half-cocked.
- Get a grasp on the most immediate problems. Then determine what should receive attention first.
- Think creatively, but look for the simplest solutions. Once the crisis is over you can work on something more elaborate and long-lasting.
- Adapt your style as needed to get through the criti-

cal period. Concentrate on achieving the results required.

You can *avoid* future crises if you:

- Expect the unexpected and prepare to handle emergencies by setting up contingency plans.
- Delegate responsibility properly and follow through on what has been delegated so there's no delay in your being alerted to problems.
- Heed the early-warning signs that enable you to act before a matter becomes urgent.

Fortunately, you can also *learn* from a crisis if you:

- Evaluate each crisis after it occurs to make sure you understand:
  1. Who or what caused the crisis.
  2. What alternative action could have or should have been taken to avoid it.
  3. What you learned from the experience that would help with similar situations in the future.

When you do these things and follow the lead of Murray, Elaine, and Roger, you'll feel in control of a situation when (at least temporarily) you can't go with your style. You'll see, as every style must, that when those circumstances happen you *can* learn to make the compromises and adjustments that will see you through the situation.

CHAPTER 17

Keeping on Track in Your Personal Style

If only I could stay organized!

By now you're aware that even if you weren't born organized, you're not doomed to a lifetime of mismatched socks and disappearing file folders.

You know you have an organizational style that's based on your natural habits. By taking charge of this style—and not really changing it—you can get and stay organized, and win your battle with time and space restrictions in the way that's right for you.

But staying organized, once you get organized, is much like staying on a diet: after the first success it's easy to get off track—especially if you're unaware of the four stages of the organizational process.

The Four Stages of the Organizing Process

Anyone who has started a diet knows that the loss of the first ten pounds is the sweet tale of success. But at the end of a fortnight or so you're not really doing as well as you did at the start. You doubt that you can keep on track the way things are currently going. And before too long you find yourself saying, "Maybe this isn't right for me. Maybe I should give up."

But giving up permanently at this stage probably means failure. Success is keeping on.

The same is true of organizing yourself—and organizing too has its stages:

Initial Stage: Euphoria.

In this stage you revel in what it's like to have control over your time or your space. You feel, "Eureka, it works!" This sense of power typically lasts two weeks.

Second Stage: Doubt and Disappointment

During this period you experience a setback. You lose something, forget an appointment, miss a deadline, or maybe see an old habit resurface.

Third Stage: Despair.

At this point you look at every setback as proof that you've failed miserably, and decide that being organized is just not in the cards for you. Even when you're highly committed, you can get off the track at this stage.

Fourth Stage: Continuation.

This is the time to get back on track. Pick yourself up and accept the fact that no matter how organized you may be, there will always be times when you mess up. Forgive yourself and continue with your new systems where you left off.

A Common Problem

As you progress you may note, to your surprise, that you can manage to stay organized in one situation but not in another. In fact, many people say that they feel more organized at work than at home (or vice versa).

Myron, for example, has a high-pressure job as a stage manager for a theater company, and because he's always on the run he has trouble staying organized on his job. But at home his life is undemanding: because he lives alone it's easier to be organized there.

Conversely, Arlene, who has a slow-paced and predictable job as a library assistant, finds she can be organized from ten to four. But as the mother of four young children, her life is chaotic at home, and as she tries to stay organized there she lives her life somewhere between stage two and three of the organizing process.

In working with persons with the problem of being more organized at work than at home (or vice versa), I've found that several factors can influence how people approach these two different areas of their lives.

1. Expectations

Someone expects you to perform according to a certain standard. That pressure is not present in the other area of your life. For example, Barry, a disc jockey and announcer for a small radio station, has no pressure to keep any order in his cubbyhole office at the studio. Papers and tapes are everywhere in complete disarray. But Barry is "tops" when he's on the air, so no one expects him to be organized or worries about his laid-back ways. His wife, however, keeps their home in next-to-perfect order, and made it clear at the start of their marriage that Barry was expected to conform. Because of her expectations he leaves his disorganization at work when he heads for home.

2. Levels of responsibility

You are responsible for many people or many facets of an operation in one area of your life but not the other. Arlene, the library assistant, had time to be organized in her job, but at home the responsibility for her small children presented a different set of demands and a constant need to switch gears.

3. Environmental conditions

You have space that is more comfortable and easier to organize in one area than it is in the other. Janet, a back-to-work woman, is so organized in her spacious home that in her converted bedroom/sewing room she has row after row of see-through plastic boxes labeled, "LARGE BUTTONS," "SMALL BUTTONS," "RIBBONS," "TAPE," and everything else within easy reach for designing and sewing her clothes. But when she returned to the fashion world as an assistant designer, the cramped space she shares with other designers is nothing short of disaster.

If it bothers you that you're organized in one place and not in another here are some things you can do:

- Examine carefully the factors influencing how you approach different areas to see what might apply to you.
- Decide if you want to upgrade your systems, either at work or at home.
- Analyze what's standing in your way.
- Read your style chapter(s) for the strategies and techniques that will improve your particular situation.

Final Reminders that Will Keep You on Track

To *stay* organized, according to your style, here are ten final suggestions.

1. Post in a prominent spot by your desk the index card which—hopefully—you used as a bookmark while reading this book.

Its message? The secret of being organized under any circumstance, and in any situation, is taking charge of your organizational styles rather than letting them take charge of you. Following this will keep your life in order on a daily basis.

2. Refresh yourself periodically on the basics for everyone.

Since every organizational style implements variations of the basic time and space principles, reread them occasionally so you can keep personalizing them for your style and individual needs.

3. Make sure your new organizational systems are built on both firmness and flexibility.

Have a solid structure to work from, but know when to be gentle with yourself. Make allowances for special circumstances and limited goof-off times. You're not a machine and you can't always perform at full capacity. Be realistic about what you can and should be expected to do, and always have a Plan B. Be prepared in case someone throws a monkey wrench into your finely tuned systems.

4. Maintain the standards you've set for yourself.

After you decide what degree of improvement you'll aim for and how much backsliding you'll tolerate, try to stay on course. It helps to actually visualize how you want to act so you can easily see when you're not heading in the right direction.

5. Keep a positive attitude and don't take yourself too seriously.

You don't have to be a Pollyanna to look for the bright side of a bad experience. Actually, it's a necessary survival technique to be able to bounce back from disappointment and failure. If you spend too much time feeling hurt, embarrassed, or angry, you're bound to miss an opportunity to improve the situation.

6. Handle frustration and anxiety as productively as possible.

When you first struggle to move forward and encounter difficult choices and risks, frustration and anxiety are almost inevitable. But they can easily impede your progress if you don't understand their roots and work toward eliminating their negative effects. Pay attention to what makes you frustrated or anxious. This will help you see if anything can be done to improve those situations. If little can be done, concentrate on what you can do to calm yourself down and make the best of things.

7. Create working and living environments that are comfortable, functional, and reflect your personal style.

Some of us have chosen to be blind to the environments we live and work in. We're so busy racing from here to there, we use our homes or offices only as way stations. But poorly organized, unattractive spaces will never have just a neutral effect on us. Without realizing it, our time and energy can be drained by environments that don't support us in what we're trying to do. Regardless of your style, the more satisfied you are with your surroundings, the more you'll be encouraged to perform at your best.

8. If you have trouble dealing with another style, learn how to really listen and make compromises while remembering that others may not yet be ready or willing to do things differently.

It can be irritating to live or work with someone who has very different ideas from you about what the word "organized" means. But to insist that your way is the right way or the best way is a sure way to create resistance to your ideas. What happens is that most of us are comfortable, or at least familiar, with the styles with which we grew up. And somehow (unless we're taught differently or we rebel) we think that what we learned at home is the way things are done. As a result, it takes patience and caring to allow for differences in others who believe that their upbringing is the way.

9. Always be alert for signs that your style is not working for you or that it may be inappropriate for the situation you're in.

Keep on top of what's working or not working and what's helping or hindering you in your efforts to be effective. Here are five warning signs that your style may not be working for you:

- You notice that the level of productivity you've maintained has fallen off significantly without your being able to pinpoint a major contributing factor (for example, deadline work on a large project, unusual stress on the job or at home, poor health, boredom, etc).
- Other people start complaining about your job performance.
- You realize that you're misplacing too many things.
- Your systems begin to develop backlogs and bottlenecks.
- You no longer feel in control.

If your style is not working for you, go back to the appropriate chapter(s) in this book and determine what approach might make things better. Implement that approach and continue to evaluate and modify it as necessary.

10. Accept that there will always be changes in your life.

Nothing stays the same. Robert Propst, the designer, put it well when he said, "People who design houses imagine that life in that setting is static. But in fact, people are forever introducing new things, holding others, disposing of others. Children grow, their needs change." Beyond the physical space that Propst refers to, there will always be other changes too—productivity followed by a lull, good times and then bad times, ups and downs. Recognize them for what they are and know that what's working for you now may not continue to work for you in the future. Above all, stay in touch with yourself so you'll be aware of when it's time to assess and update your systems.

The standards you set for yourself are up to you. But whatever they are, you can keep on track if you know:

1. What you want.
2. How to get there.
3. What you can and can't control.
4. When to relax and be kind to yourself.
5. When to push on toward your goals.

All it takes is mastering the skills that everyone can learn!

CHAPTER 18

Be Good to Yourself—
Balancing Time-Space and Life
Management

*My personal well-being and sense of balance
are as important as any of my projects and
accomplishments.*

While you master the skills for staying on track with
your organizational style, it's vital to realize that organization is a means to an end. It is not an end in itself. It
is a gateway to a *life-management* plan through which
you can develop a style of living that creates balance
and a sense of well-being that support *who you are* and
where you are in every area. It can help you open a
doorway to feeling good about yourself and attaining the
satisfying and meaningful life everyone desires.

What People Are Saying

Over the years many of my clients have told me that
even though their newly acquired organizational skills
help them get through their days and cross things off
their lists, they still feel as though they're too busy *doing*
as opposed to *being*. They feel that they're postponing
their lives while trying to get their to-do's done first.
This leads to discomfort and a sense that things are out
of balance.

"I sometimes find myself asking, 'Is this all there is?' "
said Maggie, a 32-year-old middle-school English teacher.
"From the time I was a very small child, music has been
important to me. I began plunking a neighbor's piano
when I was three years old, and by the time I was four,
my parents had me in lessons. I taught myself guitar

when I was about ten, took theory classes in high school, and played and sang in school choirs and the all-state chorus. But when high school was over, so was my formal study of music.

"I embarked on the study of education and have been happily employed as a teacher. I do quite well and I make nice money. My life is organized and manageable but overwhelmingly predictable.

"Lately I find myself grading homework and reviewing papers—and wondering whatever happened to that part of me that used to sing for joy."

Bill, a consumers' newsletter editor, put it this way: "At this point my life has become a process of solving problems and meeting deadlines. I've forgotten what it's like to catch up with myself and feel happy with who I am.

"And that's not really living."

That definitely *isn't* living, so as I worked with Maggie and Bill and many other clients who were looking beyond "Is that all?" I developed a program called The Happiness Seminar to help them reconcile their responsibilities and their passions in order to achieve a more dynamic balance in their lives.

What Is the Happiness Seminar?

Just as the organizational-styles approach has you examine what comes naturally to you so you can build from there, The Happiness Seminar invites you to explore what will bring you happiness and satisfaction so you can put more of that into your daily life. It helps people define the elements that bring them the most pleasure—yet seem to be absent from their lives. It shows them how to organize their time and space in order to start bringing those elements into play.

When your life feels out of balance, stress and burnout can be the result. You may need to start tipping the scales more evenly between:

- work/play
- seriousness/humor
- movement/stillness
- connections/solitude
- giving/receiving
- routine/variety

Understanding how to move between these poles at different times of your life—and perhaps even at different times of the day—requires an awareness of the following four steps:

1. Be who you are.
2. Be where you are.
3. Take care of yourself.
4. Give something back.

Step 1. Be Who You Are

Bill, the consumers' newsletter editor, had come far from his roots as a country boy in Texas. Well established in the field of technical publishing, he was also settling in as a new father. Although delighted with his family and career, he kept wondering why he wasn't feeling more content with where he was. At night, sitting alone on his porch and working on his laptop, he questioned what had happened to the child who used to spend hours chasing down fireflies.

I asked Bill to describe to me some scenes from his past that best illustrated to him the kind of boy he had been.

"As a kid, I loved camping out on summer nights," he said. "Stars dusted the dark Texas sky, crickets chirped, frogs croaked, and I sat up all night with my brothers and cousins. There were a thousand varieties of fun, but I loved staring at those bright stars best of all.

"On summer days it was baseball. Never cared much for watching it, but I loved to play. Afternoon games, the sun was so hot it made you dizzy, but I loved the way the heat from the sand warmed the bottoms of my cleats. And I loved cold Dr Pepper drinks, Three Musketeers bars, and sitting in the shade listening to my radio.''

Cara, a 50-year-old mother of college-age sons, was beginning to realize that she might be suffering from empty-nest syndrome. She found herself wandering from room to room in her house, picking things up and putting them down while wondering what to do with herself next. The problem was she didn't know where to start. As she spoke, it seemed to me that she had lost touch with Cara the woman, while focusing on Cara the mother and wife.

I suggested that when Cara went back home after our talk, she play a game of detective with herself and try to turn up some clues about what kind of person was living in her house now. I told her to pretend that she was entering the house for the first time and, as part of the game, try to discover everything she could about the person living in that house from what she saw in front of her.

"Doing that was absolutely fascinating," Cara said the next time that we spoke. "First of all, I felt like there were bits and pieces of me from a long time ago that had been covered up and pushed aside by 'stuff' that I don't even remember accumulating! In one closet I found half a dozen jigsaw puzzles that I haven't seen in years. And I love jigsaw puzzles.

"I discovered pictures in a drawer of a trip we took fifteen years ago to Tibet. I was so moved by the people and the scenery that I wanted—and still want—to learn more about the area. I paged through my personal phone book and saw names of people I haven't spoken to in years whom I miss. As I went through the house, I picked up handfuls of magazines that I get but am no longer interested in reading. I found an old wicker basket of yarn—and I haven't felt like knitting in years. I also saw tacky little knickknacks on the living room tables that I can't stand looking at anymore.

"I thought to myself, 'Who, exactly, is living in this house these days?' ''

Bill and Cara's Self-Discovery

As part of their self-discovery I had Bill and Cara pretend to hold a pair of binoculars to their eyes and imagine that every turn of the knob would sharpen and clarify their image of themselves. With each turn they were to ask themselves one of the following questions:

- At what times in my life have I felt most fully alive?
- What are my favorite childhood memories?
- What would I do today during an ideal day alone?

The "Things You Love" Exercise

Sit down with a pen and paper and make a list of 100 Things That Bring You Pleasure from the small ("watching my son sleep") to the large ("mountain climbing"). Keep writing without stopping, until you reach 100 even if you have to repeat entries several times. After a while you'll notice that you're starting to come up with ideas that surprise you.

3 More Tips for Sharpening Your Image of Yourself

- Start to visualize yourself as a fascinating person you'd like to know better.
- Observe your reactions to everything.
- Listen to yourself.

Step 2. Be Where You Are

It has been said that the past is history, the future a mystery, and this moment a gift. That's why it's called the present. But many of us miss the present because we're too involved in looking in other directions.

Steve, an investment banker, was one of my best-organized clients when it came to the way he handled his work. He was successful financially, and with a large mortgage on his mini-mansion home and four sons to educate, he had to earn "big money" and stick with investment banking for his foreseeable future.

"But my life is all pressure," he confessed, "and this is not where I want to be. As a boy I lived in a rural town in a little white house, and I'd love to go back to that simpler life. I'd give up my six bedrooms and seven bath-spas to have less stress and more problem-free living."

Another client, Marcia, is a single mother and children's clothing designer who has to lead an organized life to accomplish all she needs to do.

"My entire life is 'getting things done,'" she said in one of my seminars. "I'm not a bit happy with where I'm at, but I don't know how to change things."

What Steve and Marcia Can—and Needed to—Do

First, both Steve and Marcia needed to accept the reality of their situations. This meant recognizing they were currently committed to reaching certain financial goals they had set for themselves and that, to a certain extent, their daily schedules were controlled by the exigencies of making a living. Marcia had no one else to rely on to help her pay her bills. And Steve, though he claimed he was ready to cut back and simplify, was not yet at the point that he felt he could change his lifestyle dramatically.

I suggested that Steve and Marcia begin looking at what they could control as a way to balance the factors they felt were not under their control. Since their daily work schedules were predetermined, we first examined the hours when they were not at work to see how much flexibility there was. A review of time logs that they kept showed, surprisingly, that there were pockets of free time for them that they were not taking advantage of. Not for time to get more things done. But time for periods of decompression—either relaxation or stimulation that would make it easier to get back to the required to-do's.

Accepting that this time was available to them, and learning how to take advantage of it, meant that both Steve and Marcia had to understand that the present moment was the only moment they could work with. If they spent it worrying about things that had already happened or obsessing about events that hadn't yet occurred, they'd miss a golden opportunity to nourish themselves and to feel better in the process. What's required for Steve, Marcia, and all the rest of us is to recognize that the only place you can be at the moment is exactly where you are. Only from that place can you be in touch with how you're feeling, what's most important to you, and what would best contribute to your sense of well-being.

How You Can Be Where You Are— and Feel Balanced

The first secret of learning to balance your life and increase your sense of well-being without having to change too much is *controlling your attitude*. Most of us have a perspective that either *beats* us up or *builds* us up. Here are ways to *build* yourself up, no matter where you are.

- Realize that the more you can accept and appreciate the current circumstances of your life, the better position you will be in to effect change for the future. In other words, don't fight reality. Deal with it.
- Look at what's *right* with your life instead of centering primarily on what's *wrong* or not working. It's possible to learn how to be happy without changing very much except your outlook. How else do we explain people living in very difficult circumstances, some of whom become bitter and angry about what fate has dealt them, and others who make the best of what they have in gratitude for being able to have that much?

- Try viewing your day in terms of working more effectively with *people* and building better *relationships*. This is equally as important as focusing on what you can accomplish/do more quickly/or get out of doing.
- Slow down and tune up your senses to appreciate the little things and experience each moment. Very simply this means savoring the croissant with raspberry jam that's in front of you while you're eating it as opposed to having your mind elsewhere and never noticing or valuing the small pleasures you have *now*.
- Refrain from defining your well-being (or lack of well-being) in terms of the external events in your life. It's a waste of time and energy to try to fix everything on the outside with the hope of then being able to feel good on the inside. Health and well-being come from the *inside out,* so pay attention to the messages you're giving yourself.

Step 3. Take Care of Yourself

Wendy, whom everyone revered as a tireless visiting nurse, was an unhappy camper when she told me she'd actually grown to hate spending all her waking hours caring for others' needs.

"I've always been a born nurturer," she said, "so people tend to depend on me both at home and at work. I'm expected to take care of *everything,* and no one stops to think I might have my own needs, too.

"At work everyone on the staff unloads their problems on me. On visits to patients, people are demanding—and often difficult. And at home my husband and children have an ongoing list of immediate needs that always have to come first.

"I'm beginning to feel like a martyr, and it's taking a toll on me."

No one should have to feel like a martyr because of

mistakenly thinking people can fill others' needs without also filling their own.

What Wendy Needs to Rethink

When I met with Wendy, one of the first things I said to her was "Think of the last time you were in an airplane and listened to the flight attendant talk about emergency procedures. What were you told to do in the event of loss of cabin pressure and the appearance of your oxygen mask? Who should receive the oxygen first—you or whoever is traveling with you who might need assistance?"

"You, of course," answered Wendy, picking up on my cue that none of us can do very much for others if we can't breathe ourselves.

This personal breathing time each day is a must for balance, so remember to nurture yourself daily without feeling guilty about it.

5 Ways to Nurture Your Own Well-Being

- Believe that you can and must take good care of yourself. This is not selfishness.
- Ask yourself often, "What do I need to do right now to take better care of myself?"
- Tell yourself, "I deserve the same kind of care I give others." Then pay attention to your needs in the same way you pay attention to friends, colleagues, and family members.
- Know what you need to do to season your routine with small pleasures for *you* and adopt the philosophy that many of these small daily pleasures are only as far away as you make them.
- Enjoy your life.

The Happiness Continuum

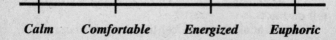

| Calm | Comfortable | Energized | Euphoric |

One way of getting in touch with what you need at the moment is to refer to the Happiness Continuum, an illustration of the range of energy levels you typically experience in your life. It provides you with a way of identifying what you may be missing or what you may need more of.

The Continuum ranges from *Calmness* on the far left through *Comfortable* to *Energized* and *Euphoric*. Begin by asking yourself what level of energy you feel most like experiencing at the moment or in the next time period you can plan for. Identify that level and then select an activity that might bring you to that desired state.

Examples:

Calm

- Watch a sunset or lie on the grass and look at the sky.
- Listen to a fountain or a flowing stream.
- Sip hot tea and watch the rain.
- Light candles and take a bath.

Comfortable

- Curl up in a blanket on a cold, snowy day.
- Eat warm cookies.
- Make a fire in the fireplace.
- Put your favorite fresh sheets on your bed.

Energized

- Open the windows and let in fresh air.
- Put on jazzy music and move.
- Rearrange your furniture.
- Ride your bike fast.
- Rent an exciting movie.

Euphoric

- Go to a loud concert.
- Dance until you're exhausted.

- Attend a hotly contested athletic match.
- Engage in a daredevil sport.

Step 4. Give Something Back

Along with (1) being *who* you are, (2) being *where* you are and (3) caring for *yourself,* it's important to (4) give something back. We're in a position to do this when we can enjoy our life and appreciate the blessings we have.

Maria, a computer programmer, was in such a position—and did something about it. Maria's mother came to the United States from abroad when Maria was a baby. Her mother struggled to provide adequately for Maria, but they lived in poverty for much of Maria's young life. There was very little bitterness, however, because Maria learned, from watching her mother, how to enjoy even the smallest blessings. Maria grew up valuing education and worked diligently to earn a scholarship to a good college. She studied hard and was able to secure a good job and, eventually, a supervisory position in computer technology.

Although her hours were full, Maria felt that something was missing from her life—that her job and personal relationships were not satisfying enough. She realized what it was when, during a visit back to the neighborhood where she had grown up, she talked to a former acquaintance who complained to Maria how difficult it was to get employment because of the language barrier.

At that moment Maria realized what she wanted to do. She knew how fortunate she had been in having a role model such as her mother, who showed her how to make the most of her talents so she could get ahead and enjoy life. Now she knew that she wanted to turn around and do the same for someone else. She located an English as a Second Language (ESL) program, became a certified instructor, and began to volunteer at the local Y as a mentor to teenage girls. Maria had found her mission.

Your Personal Mission

Every one of us has a purpose for living and a personal mission to contribute something positive to our small or large community through being who we are. This is brought home to me constantly as I work with all types of persons and observe again and again that when people aren't aware of their mission—what it is that they're uniquely qualified to contribute—they focus instead on their problems and the ways in which they're limited by those problems. Once you're conscious of your purpose, however, you develop perspective and problems become "just things to handle."

Marilyn is a retired high school teacher whose routine had become a predictable round of food shopping, errand running, hair appointments, and occasional lunches with friends. She spent considerable time each day checking the weather reports, worrying about traffic congestion, and listening to descriptions of her neighbor's ailments. Each day was a new battle with the elements. She had always assumed that happiness lay on the other side of these daily problems—that if she could just make it through the day and get done what needed to be done, then she might be able to enjoy a few moments of earned pleasure.

But if problems are your major focus, then problems will be all that you see. Marilyn decided to take a closer look at her life to discover what gave her pleasure when she wasn't looking for what could go wrong. She realized that she did enjoy hearing her friends' stories and that they considered her to be a compassionate listener. One of the friends told Marilyn about the nursing home where her mother was and how lonely the residents were when family members couldn't visit. The friend suggested that perhaps Marilyn could spend some time with the residents just chatting with them and keeping them company.

The idea seemed like a good one, and Marilyn decided to schedule a few hours a week at the home. Before long she was surprised at how much she began to look forward to the visits. Possible rainstorms and traffic jams became just nuisances to deal with on the way to her work, as opposed to significant events that she had to worry about all day. Her time and attention were spent on what was truly meaningful—the service she was providing to others and, as a result, to herself.

How to Define Your Personal Mission

You are unique, so no one else can make the same contribution as an individual that you can. Keeping this in mind, make a copy of the following worksheet to define your personal mission. Use all the space you need for each listing.

1. List your talents and interests as fully as you can.

_____

_____

_____

_____

_____

2. Write down what you consider to be your most closely held beliefs and underlying values.

_____

_____

_____

_____

_____

3. Think about possible ways these talents, interests, values, and beliefs can be combined in service activities or projects.

_____

_____

_____

_____

_____

4. Keep in mind your current time commitments and priorities while selecting one possible service activity or project that excites your imagination.

_____

_____

_____

_____

5. Write down the steps you need to take to get started on this project and begin taking those steps now to fulfill your mission.

_____

_____

_____

_____

_____

A Final Round-up for Balancing Time-Space and Life Management

1. Learn how to make your energy work for you through this "Things That Increase Your Energy/Things That Decrease Your Energy" exercise.

Be aware of what enhances your energy level and what depletes it so that you can give yourself a boost whenever you need to. For this exercise, simply make a list of those people, places, and activities that put a smile or your face, as well as those that pull you down. If you're conscious of these things, you can learn how to pair an energy drainer with an energy booster, so that you can bring yourself back up again.

2. Know where to focus your energy and attention.

Unfortunately, some people spend more time sorting out their laundry than sorting out their thoughts. Successfully managing your time, your space, and your life requires that you really listen to yourself to discover what's important to you and to check and see that things feel right. Remember, it's of no use to do something perfectly that doesn't need to be done at all, and, conversely, it can be dangerous to ignore those sides of you that need to be expressed. Take time to listen so you know what to do next.

3. Recognize there are times in your life when balance is going to be temporary imbalance.

It has been said that a successful life can be like a successful tightrope walk. Sometimes the balance pole must dip strongly one way. Sometimes it can dip gently the other way. And sometimes it's perfectly still.

There are times when a short-term focus—such as returning to school, caring for a newborn or elderly relative, starting a business, or any number of other things—

will of necessity take priority over other activities. During those periods you have to be flexible. But at some point it will be appropriate to quell the flow of adrenaline and return to a more even balance.

4. Understand that you have more control over your way of living than you think you have.

Granted, there are things you can't control—like other people's reactions and choices, the weather, computer meltdowns, and Murphy's Law. But, on the other hand, if you find yourself thinking too often that other people are controlling your life, it may well be that you're giving them permission to do so. Ultimately, you are the only one with the power to make your life work for you. This may require an attitude adjustment on your part, but it is an essential one if you're going to opt for real happiness.

5. Make it your ongoing habit to examine the boundaries you consciously or unconsciously set in your life.

There's a story about a woman and her two goldfish that she kept in a small bowl. One day she decided to give the goldfish a treat while she cleaned out their bowl. She filled up her bathtub and put the goldfish in the tub so they'd have a much larger space in which to swim. But when she returned to take them out of the tub she found them swimming around in small circles within boundaries that were the same as their bowl.

Humans obviously aren't goldfish. But how many of us set boundaries that are too limited because we perceive our worlds in certain predictable ways and forget that the boundaries we see around us are very often the ones we put there? When we break through these boundaries, however, we become like Dorothy in *The Wizard of Oz,* and realize that we have the power to go "home" to our real selves and our wide-open opportunities, whenever we choose.

In a world where the pace is ever increasing, knowing yourself is the key—whether you're an Everything Out,

Nothing Out, Right Angler, Pack Rat, Total Slob, Perfectionist Plus, Allergic to Detail, Fence Sitter, Cliff Hanger, or Hopper. When you understand your personal style, you can adapt traditional organizational practices *and* the latest technology to balance time-space and life management and create a productive and meaningful life.

Index